CW00369791

# THE NEW ATH

**New Directions in Religion and Literature**

Series Editors: Mark Knight, Roehampton University and
Emma Mason, University of Warwick

This series aims to showcase new work at the forefront of religion and
literature through short studies written by leading and rising scholars in
the field. Books will pursue a variety of theoretical approaches as they
engage with writing from different religious and literary traditions.
Collectively, the series will offer a timely critical intervention to the
interdisciplinary crossover between religion and literature, speaking to
wider contemporary interests and mapping out new directions for the
field in the early twenty-first century.

**Titles in the series include:**

*Blake. Wordsworth. Religion*
Jonathan Roberts

# THE NEW ATHEIST NOVEL

## FICTION, PHILOSOPHY AND POLEMIC AFTER 9/11

**ARTHUR BRADLEY**
**AND**
**ANDREW TATE**

continuum

**Continuum International Publishing Group**

The Tower Building            80 Maiden Lane
11 York Road                  Suite 704, New York
London SE1 7NX                NY 10038

www.continuumbooks.com

© Arthur Bradley and Andrew Tate 2010
Arthur Bradley and Andrew Tate have asserted their right under the
Copyright, Designs and Patents Act, 1988, to be identified as the Author
of this work.

All rights reserved. No part of this publication may be reproduced or
transmitted in any form or by any means, electronic or mechanical,
including photocopying, recording, or any information storage or
retrieval system, without prior permission in writing from
the publishers.

**British Library Cataloguing-in-Publication Data**
A catalogue record for this book is available from the British Library.

ISBN:  978-0-8264-4429-5 (hardback)
       978-0-8264-4629-9 (paperback)

**Library of Congress Cataloging-in-Publication Data**
A catalog record for this book is available from the Library of Congress.

Typeset by Newgen Imaging Systems Pvt Ltd, Chennai, India
Printed and bound in Great Britain by CPI Antony Rowe,
Chippenham, Wiltshire

For Bernard Beatty and Michael Wheeler

# CONTENTS

Acknowledgements                                                    viii
Series Editors' Preface                                               ix

Introduction: The New Atheist Novel                                   1
Chapter One: Ian McEwan's End of the World Blues                     16
Chapter Two: Martin Amis and the War for Cliché                      36
Chapter Three: Philip Pullman's Republic of Heaven                   56
Chapter Four: Salman Rushdie and the Quarrel over God                82
Conclusion: The Post-Atheist Novel                                  105

Notes                                                               112
Bibliography                                                        125
Index                                                               133

# ACKNOWLEDGEMENTS

First, we are very grateful to Mark Knight and Emma Mason for commissioning this book for the New Directions in Religion and Literature series and to Anna Fleming and Colleen Coalter at Continuum for seeing it through to publication.

We would also like to thank Simon Bainbridge, Mike Greaney and Abir Hamdar for taking the time to read parts of the manuscript, offering invaluable feedback and for occasionally saving us from ourselves. Our deepest gratitude goes to our wives, Abir Hamdar and Michaela Robinson-Tate, without whose love and support this book could not have been written.

A note on authorship: Arthur Bradley wrote the Introduction, Chapter One and Chapter Two; Andrew Tate wrote Chapters Three and Four while the Conclusion was written by us both. An earlier draft of some of the material presented here was published by Arthur Bradley as 'The New Atheist Novel: Literature, Religion and Terror in Amis and McEwan', in *The Yearbook of English Studies 2009*, special issue on Literature and Religion, ed. by Andrew Tate (New York: MLA, 2009).

Finally, we would like to dedicate this book to our first and best academic mentors – Bernard Beatty and Michael Wheeler – with thanks for everything they have taught us over the years. We hope they like it.

# SERIES EDITORS' PREFACE

This series of short monographs seeks to develop the long-established relationship between the disciplines of religion and literature. We posit that the two fields have always been intimately related, aesthetically, formally and theoretically, creating a reciprocal critical awareness framed by the relatively recent theo-literary thinking of figures such as Walter Benjamin, Martin Buber, Hans-Georg Gadamer and Geoffrey Hartman. Committed to reflecting on the question of how these two disciplines continue to interact, we are particularly concerned to redress the marked evasion of this relationship within existing scholarship. As Stanley Fish recently declared, religion has the capacity to 'succeed high theory and race, gender and class as the centre of intellectual energy in academe'. The books in this series are written by a group of critics eager to contribute to and read work intimate with both evolving and new religious and literary debates. Pursuing a variety of theoretical approaches to an array of literary and cultural texts, each study showcases new work on religion and literature while also speaking to wider contemporary concerns with politics, art and philosophy. In doing so, the books collectively map out new directions for the field in the early twenty-first century.

Mark Knight
Emma Mason

# INTRODUCTION: THE NEW ATHEIST NOVEL

In the early years of the third Christian millennium, Western civilization witnessed the birth of a curious cult calling itself the 'New Atheism'. It began with the appearance of four best-selling polemics against religion in as many years: Sam Harris's *The End of Faith* (2004), Daniel Dennett's *Breaking the Spell* (2006), Richard Dawkins's *The God Delusion* (2006) and, finally, Christopher Hitchens's *God Is Not Great* (2007).[1] After this first wave subsided, the work of Dawkins and company has been endlessly propagated, debated and attacked in a series of public appearances, newspaper articles, websites, television programmes and books. To be sure, the New Atheists differ considerably in expertise – Harris is a (hitherto unknown) graduate student in neuroscience; Dennett a distinguished philosopher of mind; Dawkins a well-known evolutionary biologist and Hitchens a contrarian political journalist – but what unites them all is a conviction that religious belief is not simply irrational but immoral and dangerous. Quite simply, Harris argues, all religion must be consigned to the graveyard of bad ideas: 'Words like "God" and "Allah" must go the way of "Apollo" and "Baal"' (*The End of Faith*, p. 14). From Belfast, through Belgrade, Beirut, Bombay and Bethlehem all the way to contemporary Baghdad, Christopher Hitchens is convinced of one fact: 'religion kills' (*God Is Not Great*, pp. 15–36). For Richard Dawkins, who is undoubtedly the most zealous of the New Atheist cult, the God of monotheistic religion is 'a petty, unjust, unforgiving control freak; a vindictive, bloodthirsty ethnic cleanser; a misogynistic, homophobic, racist, infanticidal, genocidal, filicidal, pestilential, megalomaniacal, sadomasochistic, capriciously malevolent bully' (*The God Delusion*, p. 51).

1

It is not our aim in this book to offer a philosophical assessment of the truth-claims of the New Atheism but something more modest and hopefully more original: an account of its *literary* reception.[2] As this introduction will make abundantly clear, however, our own position – and we write as an atheist and a Christian respectively – is aptly summarized by the liberal philosopher John Gray.[3] To be blunt, what distinguishes the New Atheism from earlier varieties of non-belief is little more than its 'intellectual crudity' (*Black Mass*, p. 189): it is a distinctly pre-Nietzschean atheism.[4] Yet, if the New Atheism is indeed distinguished mainly by the extent of its philosophical, historical and theological impoverishment, this raises the important question of *why* it has attracted such unprecedented popular attention. Even Richard Dawkins would concede that the 'New' Atheism is something of a misnomer: an informed reader would be hard-pressed to identify anything remotely original or ground-breaking about this vintage brew of eighteenth- century philosophical empiricism, nineteenth-century evolutionary biology and early twentieth-century logical and scientific positivism. Quite the contrary: there is even something unashamedly archaic about Dawkins and company's embrace of universal reason, their moralizing sermons on the dangers of Political Correctness and their contempt for what they see as the modish mumbo jumbo of postmodernism and 'New Age' philosophy. If Dawkins, Dennett, Hitchens and Harris are undoubtedly surfing some sort of cultural *Zeitgeist*, in other words, we don't think that the popular appeal of their work can be solely explained by its (somewhat *recherché*) intellectual content. What, then, *is* 'new' about the New Atheism?

To be sure, it is tempting to wonder how the New Atheists would themselves explain the popularity of their own work: could it be proof positive of the heroic march of Enlightenment against the forces of myth, error and superstition? It is hard to imagine that even they would go so far. Not only do they seem to know comparatively little about the Enlightenment tradition they claim to uphold (Dawkins and Dennett appear to think Hume and Kant were atheists) but their collective *modus operandi* is almost a parody of rational enquiry, the empirical method or the verification principle. As many critics have pointed out, the preface to Richard Dawkins's *The God Delusion* consists of one long unverified (and frankly unverifiable) speculation about a world without God: 'Imagine, with John Lennon, a world with no religion' (pp. 23–4). Quite evidently, Dawkins himself imagines such a world would also be one without suicide bombers (but what about the Marxist-Leninist Tamil Tigers or the Communists in 1980s Lebanon?), without the Israeli/Palestinian conflict (but wasn't the PLO historically a secular nationalist organization?) and even without the Northern Irish 'Troubles' (but was the IRA war against the British state really all about the Catholic doctrine of transubstantiation?). When Dawkins and Harris turn to the small matter of the atheist tyrannies of the twentieth century, it is only to explain that Hitler was probably a Catholic anyway (but wasn't he, if anything, a social Darwinist?) whereas Stalin's and Mao's atrocities had nothing to do with their non-belief (try telling that to the Orthodox Church in the Soviet Union or the people of Tibet). Perhaps – in the absence of any compelling intellectual merits – it might be more plausible to see the New Atheism as a particularly virulent species of what Dawkins famously calls a 'meme': a cultural gene that spreads through self-replication, imitation and selection.[5] Such a thesis – unverifiable though it again may be – would at least have the benefit of explaining one of the most curious aspects of the movement: its almost totally circular self-referentiality. For many new readers, what is most striking about the work of Harris, Hitchens, Dawkins, Dennett is that it is something of a closed feedback loop in which the same information, the same arguments, even the same names, shuttle around infinitely: Hume, Darwin, Bertrand Russell and – when an authority on the iniquities of Islam is required – the *éminence grise* of the Orientalists, Bernard Lewis. If anything, the voices in the New Atheist echo chamber are echoing ever louder: Dawkins and company now introduce, review, publicize and cite one another's opinions as 'evidence' with almost incestuous frequency. In the bewildering number of internet sites devoted to the movement, which faithfully reproduce every utterance by its founding members, this process of self-replication is now multiplied almost infinitely.[6]

Yet, it might be more convincing to see the New Atheism as a response to a very specific cultural and political climate: the so-called return of the religious in the supposedly secular West. Its appeal certainly makes more sense if seen against the backdrop of the spectacular and ominous rise of American Christian fundamentalism – particularly in its militant political guise as the Christian Coalition and the Moral Majority – over the last 30 years. At the time when the first New Atheist polemics began to appear (Harris's *The End of Faith* was published in 2004), the Christian Right had reached the apogee of their cultural and political power in the USA. To begin with, George W. Bush was recognizably 'one of them' – the first Born Again Christian President. His administration, which in no small measure owed its existence to Christian 'values' voters, adopted a range of 'faith-based' positions on creationism, abortion, stem-cell research and gay marriage, as well as championing government aid to religious schools and charities and appointing sympathetic judges to federal benches. Even Bush's foreign policies – staunch support for Israel in the aftermath of the failed Oslo peace accord with Palestine and, of course, the Iraq invasion of 2003 – have been seen as the result of an unholy alliance between Neo-Conservatism and Christian Zionism.[7] For the New Atheists – three of whom, it should be remembered, live and work in the USA – it is all too clear that Christian Fundamentalism's malign influence over the American political and educational system provides the main impetus for their wholesale attack on 'religion' as such. Undoubtedly, the very real fundamentalist threat to the secular enlightenment values on which the USA was founded accounts for the strident, inflated and (at least to some Western European readers) almost hysterical tone of Dawkins and company: a distinctly Churchillian rhetoric of appeasement, gathering storms and heroic resistance dominates their work (see, for example, *The God Delusion*, pp. 90–3). Just as they see no distinction between Christianity, Judaism, Islam and all the other major religions, so they accept no meaningful distinction between liberal and fundamentalist faiths: Sam Harris's diatribe is, in fact, chiefly directed against the ideal of religious tolerance, moderation and respect as the worst kind of moral relativism (*The End of Faith*, p. 15). While Dawkins maintains the pretence that all religions are equally wrong, stupid and dangerous, it is clear that his main target is almost always Christian fundamentalism: *The God Delusion* attacks intelligent design, the persecution of homosexuals and evangelical pro-life campaigners (pp. 317–48). If Christian fundamentalism is the New Atheism's main antagonist, it may also explain why the latter is itself so regularly accused of being a 'Fundamentalism' in its own right: this absolutist, all-or-nothing monolith is, as many critics have pointed out, something of a philosophical mirror image of the belief system it rejects. On the one side, Christian Fundamentalism professes faith in the inerrancy of the Bible, in the Lutheran doctrine of *sola scriptura*, in the literal truth of Genesis and the primacy of personal morality. On the other, the New Atheism offers an equally a-historical and de-contextualized reading of the Bible and the Qur'an alone, insists upon the literal falsity of Genesis and the rank immorality of a value system that bases itself on revealed religious 'truth'. In the introduction to *The God Delusion*, moreover, Dawkins even begins to sound uncannily like a Pentecostalist evangelist whose gospel offers immediate, born-again conversion: 'If this book works as I intend, religious readers who open it will be atheists when they put it down' (p. 28).

In many ways, though, the single defining political context for the New Atheism was the al-Qaeda terrorist attacks on the World Trade Center and the Pentagon on September 11, 2001. It is the rise of Islamic extremism – or perhaps just of Islam itself, for, once again, they admit of no meaningful distinction between liberals and fundamentalists – that, more than anything, puts the 'new' into the New Atheism. According to Sam Harris, he began writing *The End of Faith* on 12 September 2001 and the book actually opens with a depiction of a young Islamic suicide bomber setting out on his mission (pp. 11–12). Not only does Dawkins cite Harris's account approvingly in *The God Delusion* but he supplements it with a discussion of the allegedly Islamist motives behind the London suicide bombings of July 2005. Even the title of Christopher Hitchens's poison-pen letter to religion is, of course, an (uncharacteristically witless) rewriting of the common Muslim profession of faith 'Allāhu Akbar'. For the New Atheists, then, Islam comes to embody the irrationality, immorality and violence of religion in general: all religions may be equal in their eyes but one, it appears, is more equal than all the others. To set the tone, Harris himself cherry-picks the Qur'an (with help from Bernard Lewis and Paul Berman) to 'prove' that Islam is a religion of the sword, dedicated to permanent *Jihad* against the infidels, and determined to convert the enemy or kill him.[8] From its apparent embrace of martyrdom as a sacred duty to its alleged desire to punish apostasy with death, the Muslim religion is a monstrous anachronism in the modern age: 'It is as though a portal in time has opened, and fourteenth-century hordes are pouring into our world' (*The End of Faith*, p. 107). Such violent origins explain why Harris, Dawkins and Hitchens also see the figure of the suicide bomber – not as a modern aberration or distortion of Islam – but as the logical conclusion of the Muslim creed: 'Islam, more than any other religion human beings have devised, has all the makings of a thoroughgoing cult of death' (p. 123). While Palestinian suicide bombers may see themselves as resisting the Israeli occupation of their homeland, Harris assures us that all they are really interested in is becoming Islamic martyrs by killing infidels (p. 131).[9] What other reason could there possibly be for such attacks, after all, when 'no other nation in history faced with comparable challenges has ever adhered to a higher standard of human rights, been more sensitive to the safety of innocent civilians, tried harder to operate under the rule of law or been more willing to take risks for peace' than the State of Israel?[10] Finally, and perhaps most ominously of all, the New Atheism's championing of the forces of Enlightenment over and against Islam also constitutes an explicit ideological justification for the War on Terror: what seemed at first glance to be a bit of harmless philosophical knockabout is, with hindsight, now starting to look like the weaponization of thought. Whereas Richard Dawkins has always been a vigorous opponent of the Iraq War – and of the Christian Zionism which at least partly gave rise to it in the USA (*The God Delusion*, pp. 341–2) – Christopher Hitchens somewhat perversely supported the invasion as nothing less than a modern war against religion. Even the Iraqi dictator Saddam Hussein – an Arab secular nationalist in the Nasser mould who abolished the jurisdiction of Sharia law over everything but personal matters when he came to power – was really a dedicated Islamist, at least according to the author of *God Is Not Great*. Just like Hitchens, Sam Harris is a cheerleader for the USA's military intervention against Islamic states: 'we cannot wait for weapons of mass destruction to dribble . . . into the hands of fanatics' (*The End of Faith*, p. 151). If anything, Harris is even more gung-ho than the Bush administration: whereas the former American president ultimately envisaged a free, democratic Iraq as a model for a modern Middle East, Harris is not convinced that the region is ready for anything so new-fangled as democracy. The Islamic world is not mature enough for free and fair elections – they would just elect Islamist parties anyway – so what is required is clearly some sort of benign secular dictator, imposed, if need be, by the West itself (p. 151). This is, needless to say, exactly the same 'strong man' theory of nation-building that led the West to support the dictatorship of Saddam Hussein – our man in Baghdad – in the first place as a secularist bulwark against the spread of the Islamic Revolution, but the irony is lost on Harris. Perhaps history will not have time to repeat itself, though, because Harris is also willing (more in sorrow than in anger naturally) to entertain the prospect of a pre-emptive nuclear strike against a weaponized Islamic state: 'it may be the only course of action available to us, given what Islamists believe' (p. 129).

## 2

To our eyes, though, it is possible to detect an obscure but even more compelling reason for the massive popular appeal of the New Atheism: it constitutes a new and powerful creation mythology that – like all mythologies – performs an implicit anthropological service. For Richard Dawkins and his fellow atheists, of course, the story of the human race is the story of our liberation *from* mythology. From the immaturity of our self-imposed childhood, the human race evolves in classically Kantian terms into the adulthood of reason, truth and freedom of thought.[11] However, a certain *mythopoeia* persists throughout their writings, as even this self-aggrandizing narrative itself makes clear. If they depict themselves as heroic opponents of 'faith' per se, the New Atheist's work is in fact under-written by, and overflowing with, unverified pieties of every descrip-tion: a Neo-Lucretian reverence for nature, a Comtean scientific positivism, a Hegelian historical teleology, a Protestant-Capitalist work ethic and, finally, an entirely Judaeo-Christian belief in the excep-tional place of the human race at the centre of all these schemas. In Mary Midgely's view, the theory of evolution even represents a quasi-religious 'cosmic mythology' that tells a 'powerful folk-tale' about the origin of life.[12] What, then, is the New Atheist creation myth?

It is understandable, of course, that a group of evolutionary biolo-gists, cognitive neuroscientists and ex-Trotskyite historical material-ists should be anxious to prove that they are not simple reductionists, but at times the New Atheists begin to resemble the New Age gurus they so despise. After disposing of the three Abrahamic religions as so much dangerous hogwash, the last chapter of Sam Harris's *The End of Faith* is surprisingly devoted to what, with Zen-like serenity, he calls 'the wisdom of the east': Buddhist mysticism, meditation, fasting and other consciousness-transforming rituals and practices. Not only is Buddhism impervious to the metaphysical illusions that plague the other ancient religions, he alleges, but it actually consti-tutes a 'rigorously empirical document' about the phenomenon of consciousness that is unmatched by anything contemporary science has to offer (p. 217). For Harris, in fact, Eastern mysticism is an entirely 'rational experience' because, in his ecstatic state of self-surrender, the mystic 'has recognised something about the nature of consciousness': it is a mode of being-in-the-world that exists prior to the Cartesian dualism of subject and object (p. 221). If Harris's faith in Buddhism is doubtless very comforting, it does lead us to wonder whether he has been reading his own book: what, for instance, is the Buddhist doctrine of reincarnation if not precisely one of those irrational metaphysical dogmas he elsewhere scorns? Perhaps one might expect that a student of neuroscience could find more plausible neuro-psychological explanations for the self-annihilating oneness with the universe described by the mystics: sensory deprivation, lack of food and water, drug-induced hallucinations. Such, though, is the blindness of faith.

For the rest of the New Atheists, it is safe to say that the 'wisdom of the East' holds rather less appeal than it does for the mystical Harris, but this does not mean that they are any more immune to the temptation of mythologizing their own non-belief. It is to say the least curious that a group of thinkers who, quite rightly, rail against the creationist assumption that humanity is at the centre of a universe that has been intelligently designed just for us should succumb so totally to anthropocentrism. As a result, evolutionary biology is imperceptibly mythologized into nothing more than a story about humanity's capacity to transcend its genetic origins and obtain rational self-mastery: the origin of species is turned into the *Bildungsroman* of the human race. To start with, of course, Richard Dawkins is relentless in his exposure of human beings as nothing but gene machines – 'what on earth do you think you are, if not a robot?' (*The Selfish Gene*, pp. 270–1) – but, as John Gray has argued, Dawkins frequently over-steps the mark of his own Darwinism to assert that human beings, uniquely among animals, can defy the laws of natural selection (*Black Mass*, p. 188). Just as Dawkins finds a Cartesian ghost in the gene machine, so Daniel Dennett, too, locates within the human species a heroic capacity to turn its back on biology: 'we have . . . the ability to transcend our genetic imperatives' (*Breaking the Spell*, p. 4). Such mythologizing gestures about selfish genes, Mother Nature's stinginess and humanity's unique capacity to overcome all genetic obstacles can be found throughout the work of the New Atheists: agency, intentionality, rationality and even morality are tautologically attributed to the very evolutionary forces that supposedly give rise to them in the first place.[13] Perhaps Dawkins and company would object that we should not read such language literally – that it is merely a colourful set of metaphors or analogies to help the layman understand – but this is not a courtesy that they extend to, say, the author of the Book of Genesis. In *The God Delusion*, humanity's capacity to defy its evolutionary biology can still be explained in evolutionary terms – free will, rationality, sexual desire, altruism, empathy and pity are really just 'misfirings' of the genetic engine (*The God Delusion*, pp. 241–67) – but this does not explain why such misfirings need to be consistently depicted as a humanist triumph of the will: 'We, alone on earth, can rebel against the tyranny of the selfish replicators' (*Selfish Gene*, pp. 200–1).[14]

Perhaps the most visible sign of the *mythopoeia* of the New Atheism, though, is the narrative form in which it is written. It is revealing, for instance, that Richard Dawkins is now best known not for his contributions to evolutionary biology 30 years ago – the selfish gene, memetics and so on – but as the creator of a best-selling publishing genre: popular science. Today, he is championed as much for his gifts as a writer – wit, clarity, story-telling, a sheer inability to write a dull page – as for the substance of his arguments.[15] One can easily find similar claims for the literary merits of Harris, Dennett and, particularly, Hitchens. Yet, the New Atheism's aesthetics are not merely a stylistic adornment; rather, they go to the very heart of their project. Not only must evolutionary biology be recognized as irrefutably true, but it must also be universally acknowledged as beautiful, awe-inspiring and even poetic. To be sure, this is, in itself, nothing new: Charles Darwin himself famously claimed to find 'grandeur' in the theory of evolution.[16] For Dawkins, however, it has become *de rigueur* to wax lyrical about, say, the 'breathtaking poetry of modern cosmology' (whatever that means) even amidst attacks on the 'fairy story' that is monotheism.[17] From *Unweaving the Rainbow* (written in response to Keats's dictum that Newton destroyed the beauty of the rainbow by explaining it) to the final chapter of *The God Delusion* (which attempts to debunk the argument that religion offers artistic inspiration), Dawkins is persistently concerned to *aestheticize* the truth claims of evolutionary biology quite independently of their empirical truth-value. If anything, Daniel Dennett leaves popular science behind altogether and heads off into the speculative realm of creation myth: he is happy to admit that his own natural history of religion is not the result of painstakingly examining the fossil record, but rather of 'extrapolating back to human prehistory with the aid of biological thinking' (*Breaking the Spell*, p. 4). This is, to say the least, a novel way to set about 'breaking the spell' religion has cast over the origin of humanity. In many ways, of course, the New Atheism's ability to tell a good story certainly helps to explain its popular appeal, but the fact remains that science and art make somewhat uneasy bedfellows. Who cares, frankly, whether evolution has grandeur? How can we scientifically prove the existence of 'beauty'? Why use concepts like beauty, poetry or narrative to explain something as non-linear, material and non-anthropocentric as natural selection?

## 3

For us, the New Atheists' desire to create a new *mythos* might also explain why they are so interested in *literature*: what starts out as science-as-novel could almost be said to reach its logical conclusion in the novel-as-science. It is not simply that Dawkins and company have clearly learnt a lot from literature: aesthetics, rhetoric, narrative. At a deeper level, we will see how the New Atheists also hold up the literary as a privileged instance of their idea of a natural, secular experience of beauty, wonder and transcendence. To Christopher Hitchens's jaundiced eyes, for instance, it seems that the novel represents just about the only religion in which it is still possible to believe. Hitchens revealingly dedicates *God Is Not Great* to the novelist Ian McEwan because the latter's body of fiction 'shows an extraordinary ability to elucidate the numinous without conceding anything to the supernatural' (p. 286). He also writes in the introduction to an anthology of atheist writings that 'as a source of ethical reflection and as a mirror in which to see our human dilemmas reflected, the literary tradition is infinitely superior to the childish parables and morality tales, let alone the sanguine and sectarian admonitions, of the "holy" books'.[18] Just as the New Atheists praise contemporary novelists, so the novelists repay the compliment: Ian McEwan is a long-standing admirer of Dawkins, Harris, Hitchens and Dennett and much of his recent work – *Saturday* (2005) and *On Chesil Beach* (2007) – could even be said to be inspired by their thought. If it is possible to argue that the novel was always secular in origins – 'the epic of a world that has been abandoned by God' in Georg Lukács's famous phrase – what we seem to be dealing with here is a new and intensely polemicized phase in the relation between fiction and non-belief.[19] In a very literal sense, it seems that we can now begin to speak of something called the 'New Atheist novel'.

What, then, *is* the New Atheist novel? Who are its leading practitioners? Why has it come into existence here, now? It is the aim of this book to trace the literary reception of the New Atheism in the work of four canonical contemporary novelists: Ian McEwan, Martin Amis, Philip Pullman and Salman Rushdie. As we will see, all four have expressed support – whether enthusiastically or more guardedly – for the New Atheism in one form or another: McEwan and Amis have written and spoken admiringly of Dawkins, Dennett, Hitchens and Harris on many occasions; Pullman has published an appreciative essay on Dawkins whereas Rushdie has made public comments in support of Hitchens. However, the New Atheist novel is much more than simply a fictionalization of the peculiar cluster of beliefs – militant atheism, evolutionary biology, neuroscience and even political Neo-Conservatism – that make up the New Atheist creed. To McEwan and his contemporaries, the contemporary novel represents a new front in the ideological war against religion, religious fundamentalism and, after 9/11, religious terror. Quite simply, the novel apparently stands for everything – free speech, individuality, rationality and even a secular experience of the transcendental – that religion seeks to overthrow. On the one hand, McEwan and his contemporaries pursue the New Atheist critique of religion, fundamentalism and terror: Islam, in particular, and religion, in general, are consistently depicted as irrational, immoral and, in their purest forms, violent. On the other, the New Atheist novelists affirm what we have seen to be the secular pieties of Dawkins et al.: evolutionary biology, scientific enlightenment and a neo-romantic celebration of the aesthetic imagination. For McEwan and company, the novel even represents a kind of secular object of devotion: it offers a this-worldly experience of grandeur, consolation, freedom and even redemption. Just as the New Atheists see literature as the acceptable face of transcendence, in other words, so the New Atheist novelists celebrate the novel form, in particular, as the basis for a humanist piety. If the New Atheist novel exhibits many of the strengths of its philosophical equivalent, however, we will argue that it demonstrates many of the latter's well-documented intellectual, political and theological blind spots. In what follows, we will argue that (for all its claims to champion freedom of thought, action and expression) what defines the

New Atheist novel is really a disturbing aesthetico-political dogmatism – about science, about reason, about religion and, in many cases, about Islam.

Chapter One explores the fiction of Ian McEwan. It is safe to say that McEwan is the leading exponent of the New Atheist novel: his fiction has always addressed scientific themes – evolution, game theory and neuroscience – but in the aftermath of 9/11 it has become increasingly antagonistic towards militant religion. According to the novelist, the terrorist attacks that day represented, above all, a failure of the moral imagination: the hijackers would not have been able to carry out their attacks if they could only have put themselves in the position of their victims.[20] However, McEwan's fiction makes clear that this critique of the solipsism of religious extremism is also a defence of the morality of the novelistic imagination. Quite simply, the novel is the place where all of us imagine what it is like to be someone else. To McEwan's eyes, then, the New Atheist novel represents a (tentative) profession of faith in the secular redemption offered by fiction itself: the novel represents the only narrative of transcendence in which we can still safely believe. If McEwan's fiction seeks to oppose literature and religion, however, we will see that this faith is tested almost to destruction in *Atonement* (2002), *Saturday* (2005) and *On Chesil Beach* (2007): what is remarkable about his depictions of the literary imaginary is how closely it resembles the religious imaginary it claims to oppose. In McEwan's version of the New Atheist novel, our faith in literature is revealed to be no more rational – and even no less dangerous – than any other faith.

Chapter Two turns to the recent work of Martin Amis. It is with Amis that we encounter the New Atheist novel in its most militant ideological form: *The Second Plane* (2008), his recent collection of essays on 9/11, has provoked a storm of protest for its critique of Islam. Like his friend Ian McEwan, Amis attempts to pit literature over and against the forces of religious extremism and, in particular, 'Islamist' terror. On the one hand, the literary imagination stands for freedom, originality and independence of mind. On the other, the Islamist imaginary is consistently depicted as dependent, circular and cliché-ridden. For Amis, then, the New Atheist novel comes to resemble what we might almost call an 'aesthetic' front in the War against Terror: the ideological struggle between literature and religion is subtly transformed into the clash of civilizations between East and West. Just as with McEwan's *Atonement* and *Saturday*, though, what is remarkable about *The Second Plane* is the number of intriguing *parallels* it draws between the novelistic and terroristic imagination: Islamic terror is not simply a closed loop of endlessly circulating clichés, Amis recognizes, but a new, horrifying and essentially creative rhetorical force. If McEwan saw 9/11 as the work of people with no imagination, Amis immediately recognizes that it actually represented an astonishing *coup de theatre* of symbolic violence that is akin to the world of the novel. In Amis's New Atheist novel, the terrorist himself is transformed into a kind of novelist.

Chapter Three examines Philip Pullman's controversial sequence of fantasy novels, *His Dark Materials* (1995–2000). Pullman, an acclaimed and innovative writer of children's fiction, is one of Britain's leading advocates of religious scepticism. Appropriately enough, his work is openly indebted to eighteenth- century Romantic atheism and he has contributed an essay to a collection in honour of Richard Dawkins. To be sure, Pullman's controversial trilogy is one of the most vivid and one-sided critiques of Judaeo-Christian theology to be articulated in recent popular culture. Just as C. S. Lewis's Narnia series, for which Pullman has a particular antipathy, may have indicated British society's debt to Christianity during the 1950s, the popularity of *His Dark Materials* signifies a more widely accepted antagonism to the Church in the early years of the twenty-first century. Yet, the trilogy has its origins in the very tradition that it critiques, since it is an explicit rewriting of one of the epics of Christian literature, John Milton's *Paradise Lost* (1667). If Pullman's hostility to Christianity is explicit, many Christians – including the current Archbishop of Canterbury – have observed that *His Dark Materials* remains aesthetically and ethically rooted in the texts against which it writes: the Judaeo-Christian scriptures. For Pullman, then, the New Atheist novel thus becomes a self-consciously heretical re-narration of such pivotal biblical events as the fall and the war in heaven which consistently appeals to Christian concepts of grace, redemption and personal sacrifice.

Finally, Chapter Four turns to the recent fiction of Salman Rushdie. It is, of course, difficult to write about Rushdie without reference to the *fatwa* that was declared against him on 14 February 1989 by Ayatollah Khomeini of the Islamic Republic of Iran. One might even argue that *The Satanic Verses* (1988) – which has come to symbolize the rivalry between artistic freedom and religious authority in the modern world – is the first New Atheist novel. Yet, its author – who was raised as a Muslim but now describes himself as 'a wholly secular person'[21] – writes about faith with a vivid imaginative sympathy that outstrips literary contemporaries like Amis and McEwan. For Rushdie, what might be called the 'quarrel over God' – to quote one of the central figures in his tenth novel *The Enchantress of Florence* (2008) – is ongoing and potentially infinite. If he shares Amis and McEwan's faith in fiction as a free imaginative space, this is a space in which religious voices are also permitted to speak. In Rushdie's own version of the New Atheist novel, fiction is less the soapbox for dogma or polemic than a utopian 'place of disputation where everything could be said to everyone by anyone on any subject, including the non-existence of God and the abolition of kings'.[22]

In *The New Atheist Novel: Fiction, Philosophy and Polemic after 9/11*, then, we seek to offer the first critical study of this new hybrid literary genre. It goes without saying that we owe a huge intellectual debt to the New Atheists themselves – Richard Dawkins, Daniel Dennett, Sam Harris and Christopher Hitchens – without whose (shall we say provocative?) work this book could not have been written. As will be abundantly clear even from this short introduction, however, what follows is not always a neutral or dispassionate discussion that subscribes to the normal codes of academic *politesse*. On the contrary, it is a critical – at times very critical – intervention in a developing field. To be sure, we find much to admire in the recent work of Ian McEwan, Martin Amis, Philip Pullman and Salman Rushdie: it would scarcely be worth writing about them at such length if we did not. Rushdie, in particular, deserves praise for the depth, complexity and generosity of his engagements with Islam when he, more than any other novelist, has grounds for attacking it. However, we also find much in the New Atheist novel that is ignorant, disturbing and – particularly in its treatment of Islam – even repugnant. What other word could we use, for example, to describe Martin Amis's casual dismissal of approximately 1.5 billion people as lacking in curiosity?[23] If we see no point in treating such claims with anything other than the contempt they deserve, this does not, of course, guarantee the accuracy or legitimacy of our own readings, which are obviously a matter for the reader's own judgement. Perhaps *The New Atheist Novel* will have been worth writing if it succeeds, not in convincing the reader one way or another of its own importance, but simply in provoking an increasingly urgent *debate* about the quality of our public intellectual discourse on religion. Why does the New Atheist novel exist? What do its exponents believe and disbelieve? Where does this new direction in literature and religion come from and – more importantly – where will it take us in the future? Let us now try to set that debate in motion.

## CHAPTER ONE

# IAN McEWAN'S END OF THE WORLD BLUES

In many ways, Ian McEwan is the New Atheist novelist *par excellence*. It is tempting to say that – if his fiction did not already exist – Dawkins and company would have had to invent it, so completely does it vindicate their world view. As he has made clear in recent articles, essays and interviews, McEwan is a committed atheist; an articulate and reasonable opponent of medieval superstitions about 'sky gods'; and, of course, a fully paid up member of the Dawkins, Dennett, Hitchens and Harris mutual appreciation society.[1] Yet, what makes McEwan a New Atheist novelist – as opposed to just one more writer who happens not to believe in God – is his readiness to proselytize on behalf of this new, secular belief system. To McEwan's eyes, a title like 'Atheist' does not begin to cover his own position precisely because it defines him according to what he does not believe as opposed to what he does. If we no longer believe in a supernatural God, he told a recent interviewer, this is, in itself, not enough: it is crucial that we go on to assert our 'belief in moral values and in love and in the transcendence that [we] might experience in landscape or art or music or sculpture' (*The New Republic*). For McEwan, as we will see throughout this chapter, it may be that his own work represents a – fragile, sceptical and always questioning – profession of faith in just this possibility of secular transcendence: what fills the place of belief in God in his own fictional world is, as he describes, belief in family, love, scientific progress and, most importantly, art. Perhaps the greatest profession of faith in McEwan's fiction, though, is its faith in fiction itself: the novel is the only utopian space where believers of every persuasion – Christians, scientists, communists, poets, even the pathologically deluded – can exist together without violence. Why, though, should a New Atheist have *faith* in anything, let alone the novel?

# 1

In his recent essay 'End of the World Blues' (2007), which is included in Christopher Hitchens's anthology of atheist literature, McEwan casts a cool New Atheist eye over religious faith: religion is by its very nature irrational, he declares, and in its more extreme messianic or apocalyptic forms, it tips over into a totalitarian pathology.[2] 'It is not for nothing', he writes of the cult leader David Koresh, 'that one of the symptoms in a developing psychosis, noted and described by psychiatrists, is "religiosity"' ('End of the World Blues', p. 365). To McEwan's way of thinking, what drives such apocalyptic prophecies of the end of the world is a deep human need to make sense of a chaotic, indifferent universe by transforming it into a narrative:

> [P]erhaps we glimpse here something in our nature, something of our deeply held notions of time, and our own insignificance against the intimidating vastness of eternity, or the age of the universe – on the human scale there is little difference. We have need of a plot, a narrative to shore up our irrelevance in the flow of things. (p. 357)

Yet, what is most characteristic of McEwan's New Atheism is not his idea of religion so much as of science: what is taking place here is not just a straightforward battle between truth and falsehood, reason and unreason. Science does not expose our desire for narrative as some kind of infantile superstition, McEwan argues, so much as attempt to tell a different, and better, kind of story. While the religious story of origins is suspect precisely because it *is* a story – because it imposes an anthropocentric narrative order upon the non-linear flux of the universe – we do not seem to have any way of understanding the universe *outside* of narrative: science will never be widely accepted as true until it attains the status of mythology. For McEwan, just as for Richard Dawkins, then, the New Atheism is not so much about exploding creation myths as *perfecting* them:

> Scientific method, scepticism, or rationality in general, has yet to find an overarching narrative of sufficient power, simplicity, and wide appeal to compete with the old stories that give meaning to people's lives. Natural selection is a powerful, elegant and economic explicator of life on earth in all its diversity, and perhaps it contains the seeds of a rival creation myth that would have

the added power of being true – but it awaits its inspired synthe-siser, its poet, its Milton. (p. 360)

If we are still awaiting the poet laureate of evolution, it seems that, in the meantime, we can take consolation from what poetry we do have: McEwan's essay goes on to cite Philip Larkin's late lyric 'Aubade' as a 'supreme secular meditation on death' that stands in contrast to the feverish end-time visions of Judaeo-Christian and Islamic escha-tology (p. 352). Just as Hitchens sees McEwan as the novelist of the non-supernatural numinous, then, so McEwan himself holds up Larkin as 'an atheist who also knew the moment and the nature of transcendence' (p. 363). In this sense, we can begin to glimpse why the novel, in particular, and literature, in general, is so intrinsic to McEwan's atheism: it offers an End of the World Blues – an epic narrative of birth, death and transcendence – in which we can all believe.

It is, of course, possible to trace McEwan's interest in what we might call the human 'will-to-narrative' story back through his liter-ary career. After all, *Black Dogs* (1992) is in many ways a fictional version of 'End of the World Blues': the novel stages the exact same rhetorical struggle between science and religion through the story of a marriage breakdown in post-war Britain. For Jeremy, the agnostic narrator of the text, the battle between religion and science, mysti-cism and materialism, reason and unreason, is embodied by his estranged parents-in-law, June and Bernard Tremaine:

> Rationalist and mystic, commissar and yogi, joiner and abstainer, scientist and intuitionist, Bernard and June are the extremities, the twin poles along whose slippery axis my own unbelief slithers and never comes to rest.[3]

However, what Jeremy quickly discovers is that the two apparent extremities represented by June and Bernard actually meet in the middle: we are not dealing with a struggle between myth and reason but, once more, between two equally potent narratives of redemp-tion. On the one hand, June's Damascene conversion to religion following a terrifying encounter with two enormous black dogs is not as irrational as it first seems: her retreat into spiritual quietism is (surprisingly and generously) depicted as a dignified response to the deep trauma of the twentieth century. On the other, though, Bernard's own scientific materialism comes uncomfortably close to blind faith: he remains a member of the Communist Party right up until the invasion of Hungary in 1956 before making the predictable journey rightwards from Labour MP to Garrick club elder statesman. Both husband and wife, it seems, are equally guilty of the charge of myth-making, of story-telling, of bending the facts to fit their own position (*Black Dogs*, pp. 88–9). If Jeremy himself vacillates between the twin poles of June and Bernard's self-serving narratives – rightly suspecting their shared certainty that they alone are right – what remains revealingly constant throughout the text is his commitment to the redemptive power of narrative itself. We learn that our narrator is attempting to redeem his own shattered personal history by constructing a new (and equally self-serving) meta-narrative in the form of a family memoir: 'I would be false to my own experience if I did not declare my belief in the possibility of love transforming and redeeming a life' (p. 20). Just as 'End of the World Blues' speaks of our deep human need for story, so, here, too it seems that there is no way out of what Jeremy dismissively calls the 'necessary mechanism' whereby a life is 'reduced to, traduced by, a plot': a 'morality must be distilled from a sequence of actions' and 'an audience must be sent home with something unforgettable to mark a character's growth' (p. 50). Perhaps this is the ultimate significance of the mysterious encounter with the black dogs that doom Bernard and June's marriage almost before it has begun: what seems to matter to McEwan is not their 'real' historical meaning – June immediately interprets them as the embodiment of human evil whereas Bernard just as self-servingly dismisses this as mere superstition – so much as the impossibility of us reading them as anything *other* than meaningful.

According to many critics, though, it is *Enduring Love* (1997) that perfects what we might a little glibly call the McEwan formula: 'scientific-rationalist-hero-realises-world-more-complicated-place-than-previously-thought'.[4] It is striking that this realisation is once again accompanied by the revelation that the supposedly disinterested scientist is no more immune to the virus of narrative than his literature-loving wife or even the religious lunatic who stalks him. To Joe Rose, a frustrated scientist turned popular science journalist, the narrative mode in which he is compelled to write seems to be little more than a Victorian literary anachronism which has no place in the modern era:

> It was the nineteenth-century culture of the amateur that nourished the anecdotal scientist . . . The dominant artistic form was the novel, great sprawling narratives which not only charted private fates, but made whole societies in mirror image and addressed the public image of the day . . . Storytelling was deep in the nineteenth-century soul.[5]

Yet, once again, the supposedly archaic desire to tell and be told a story is more resilient than we might think: our narrator himself is forced to admit that twentieth-century sciences like psychoanalysis and anthropology are themselves 'fabulation run riot' (*Enduring Love*, p. 50). Even Joe's own account of the decline and fall of the narrative form in the age of Einsteinian theoretical science is, of course, a 'narrative in itself': it is not written 'in pursuit of truth' but of 'readability' and an equally compelling case could be made that the twentieth century represented the 'summation' of narrative in science (pp. 48–51). For Joe, then, just as for Jeremy in *Black Dogs*, the ideological struggle between fact and myth, reason and unreason, quickly unravels into a struggle between two competing mythologies of redemption in which objective truth is beside the point. 'We're descended from the indignant, passionate tellers of half truths', he recognizes, 'who in order to convince others, simultaneously convinced themselves' (p. 181). Finally, and most disturbingly, though, *Enduring Love* confronts us with the most indignant and passionate story-teller in McEwan's fiction: Joe's deluded, born-again stalker Jed Parry. Jed is almost a pathological narratologist insofar as he is incapable of encountering anything – even or especially the random, contingent or meaningless – without transforming it into a chapter in a longer story of redemption: 'You had to be leading me on for a reason', he tells the utterly oblivious object of his devotion, 'You were called to God and you were fighting it and you seemed to be asking me to help you' (p. 210). If Jed embodies McEwan's belief that the human desire for narrative can turn into a kind of quasi-religious pathology – where the patient comes to believe that they are the subject of a divinely preordained plan – what is striking here is that, once again, there is no possibility of an entirely *de-narrated* position. Perhaps it is no accident that one of the recurring nightmares in his work (think of Briony at the end of *Atonement* or Baxter and Henry's mother in *Saturday*) is the loss of memory: the de-narrated self is also the dehumanized self.[6] While it would be going too far to say that *Enduring Love* sees *everything* as just story (McEwan is, like the rest of his New Atheist comrades, a sternly moralizing critic of the supposed fripperies of postmodern relativism), reading the novel is akin to opening a never-ending series of Russian dolls: what is apparently the most authoritative, least fictional account of all – the medical case history which stands outside the main narrative as an appendix – is, famously, a scholarly forgery perpetrated by McEwan himself (pp. 233–43).[7] In his pre-September 11 fiction, then, it seems that McEwan remains deeply sceptical about the right of any one narrative to monopolize reality – *Black Dogs* is broadly sympathetic to June's religious conservatism while *Enduring Love* ironically reveals Joe's scientific rationalism to have been right all along – but what emerges even more clearly is his belief that, as human beings, we can have no experience of the real outside narrative.

2

In many ways, it is tempting to see September 11, 2001 as the crux upon which the later McEwan's literary career turns. It is the freak, aleatory event – the black dogs – to which his own desire for narrative order must respond. According to Theo Tait, McEwan was uniquely placed among novelists to write about the post-September 11 world – with its queasy atmosphere of fear, paranoia and impending doom – for the very good reason that he had already written about it before it happened: 'The prevailing public mood has come to resemble closely that of an Ian McEwan novel'.[8] However, what is clearly intended as praise of McEwan's earlier novels could just as easily be read as an indictment of the more recent work. To put it bluntly, what is remarkable about McEwan's post-9/11 fiction is how *little*, rather than how much, it changes. From a freak ballooning accident in *Enduring Love*, we move seamlessly to a terrorist attack which kills thousands in *Saturday*, but both are little more than structural McGuffins that exist in order to let the author stage a by now very well-rehearsed debate between science and religion, idealism and materialism and so on. Perhaps the only significant change from the earlier work is a growing interest in the moral status of the novel itself. If McEwan remains as sceptical than ever of the End of the World Blues – and what he calls 'Islamism' is, of course, a convenient target here – his later fiction professes a fragile but increasingly visible faith that the novel form itself is uniquely equipped to deal with, give room to and interrogate the various belief systems that compete to narrate and explain our world. What form, then, does this faith take?

To our eyes, McEwan's belief in the redemptive powers of the literary can be traced back to his affecting response to September 11 in an article entitled 'Only Love Then Oblivion' that was published four days after the attacks.[9] McEwan begins the essay by describing how the horrifying images he saw on his television set continued to haunt his imagination: 'Waking up before dawn, going about our business during the day, we fantasise ourselves into the events. What if it was me?' According to the novelist, though, this act of imagining – of putting ourselves in the position of others – is precisely what separates us from the terrorists. For McEwan, it is empathy (where we imagine what it must have been like to be on those hijacked planes or in those burning buildings) that constitutes morality:

> Imagining what it is like to be someone other than yourself is at the core of our humanity. It is the essence of compassion, and it is the beginning of morality. (Only Love Then Oblivion)

What if it was me? If the hijackers had been able to imagine themselves into the position of the passengers, they would not have been able to do what they had done: 'It is hard to be cruel once you permit yourself to enter the mind of your victim'. Perhaps this is true but, nonetheless, there is something unconvincing about McEwan's attempt to pit the moral imagination against the forces of terror: James Wood, who is normally a sympathetic reader of the novelist, goes so far as to call it 'liberal wish-fulfillment'.[10] In a paradoxical sense, though, 'Only Love Then Oblivion' suffers not from an excess of imagination – of wishfulness – but a shortfall: it lacks the very quality of empathy (for the attackers as well as the victims) that it upholds as the essence of morality. What if Mohammed Atta *did* imagine the deaths of his American victims? What if his motives were slightly more complex than 'fanatical certainty, misplaced religious faith and dehumanising hatred'? What if, as most observers now agree, the attacks of September 11 were entirely conceived as *symbolic*

– which is to say imaginative – acts of violence? Such, it seems, are the limits of McEwan's own moral imagination.

So what, then, is the essay on September 11 really about? It is possible to argue that McEwan's text is best read, not as a political or philosophical explanation of terror, but as the beginning of a sustained reflection upon the role, obligations and limitations of the *novel*. According to the author himself, the novel form best encapsulates the transformation described in 'Only Love Then Oblivion' because fiction is the place where all of us – whether as writers or readers – imagine what it is like to be someone else. In a 2002 interview about his novel *Atonement*, McEwan goes on to say that this capacity to inhabit other minds is what makes the novel – more than any other work of art – a moral space:

> I think, of all literary forms, and perhaps of all artistic forms, it is the most adept at showing us what it is like to be someone else. The novel is famously good at revealing, through various literary conventions, a train of thought, or a state of mind. You can live inside somebody else's head. Within one novel you can live inside many different people's heads, in a way that you of course cannot do in normal life. I think that quality of penetration into other consciousnesses lies at the heart of its moral quest. Knowing, or sensing what it's like to be someone else is at the foundations of morality.[11]

For us, McEwan is beginning to draw the battle lines of the New Atheist novel here and this war is played out throughout his post-9/11 fiction: *Atonement*, *Saturday* and *On Chesil Beach*. On the one hand, we have the literary imagination that enables us to inhabit the minds of others and thus to respect them as distinct from our own. On the other, we have the religious or terrorist consciousness that is quite unable to step outside its own solipsistic world view. If McEwan's almost Victorian faith in the amelioratory power of the novel will strike many readers as even more naïve than his explanation of terrorism – does he believe that the September 11 attacks would not have happened if Mohammed Atta had only put down the Qur'an and read *Middlemarch* instead? – it is a testament to the sophistication of his fiction that this credo is continually tested, challenged and problematized in the works that follow. To what extent, McEwan's fiction asks, is a quasi-religious faith in the novel any more rational – or any less dangerous – than religious faith itself?

## 3

In *Atonement* (2002), a novel completed before September 11, McEwan tests his faith in the morality of the literary imagination almost to destruction. As an exceptionally precocious young girl, the book's anti-heroine Briony Tallis ponders what Anglo-Saxon philosophers euphemistically call the 'problem' of other minds: 'was everyone really as alive as she was?'[12] On the one hand, the question confronts her with the possibility of 'an unbearably complicated' world with 'everyone's thoughts striving in equal importance, and everyone's claim on life as intense, and everyone thinking they were unique when no one was' (*Atonement*, p. 36). On the other, though, the question also throws up the prospect of a world in which 'she is surrounded by machines, intelligent and pleasant enough on the outside, but lacking the bright and private *inside* feeling she had' (p. 36). However, the problem of other minds ceases to be a simply academic one when Briony happens to observe a sexually charged encounter between her elder sister Cecilia and the housekeeper's son, Robbie. For the mature Briony, this childhood moment represents the beginning of her own career as a novelist because it is the first time she truly realizes that other people do exist:

> She need not judge. There did not have to be a moral. She need only show separate minds, as alive as her own, struggling with the idea that other minds were equally alive. It wasn't only wickedness and scheming that made people unhappy, it was confusion and misunderstanding; above all, it was the failure to grasp the simple truth that other people are as real as you. And only in a story could you enter these different minds and show how they had an equal value. That was the only moral a story need have. (p. 40)

From the childhood world of fairy tales – with its perfectly symmetrical distribution of beautiful heroines and wicked witches – Briony moves to the darker, more ambiguous and distinctly adult world of the novel. If a novel does not need to moralize about other minds – to judge them good or evil – it is because, as we have seen, it is *itself* a moral experience of those minds: *le roman, c'est les autres.*

Perhaps more interestingly still for a post-September 11 audience, though, Briony's newly awakened moral awareness of the lives of others also carries with it a sensitivity to an imminent threat. Reading the encounter between Robbie and Cecilia wrongly, the young girl mistakes sexual arousal as male aggression: 'Something irreducibly human, or male, threatened the order of their household, and Briony knew that unless she helped her sister, they would all suffer' (p. 114). Just as McEwan opposes the moral imagination to the solipsistic terrorist in 'Only Love Then Oblivion', so in *Atonement*, too, the novelistic sensitivity to other minds is pitted against something 'elemental, brutal, perhaps even criminal' (pp. 113–14) that endangers those minds. In both cases, the novelist asks the question that, in their own minds at least, never occurs to the terrorist: what must it feel like to be a victim?

To our eyes, though, what is most intriguing about *Atonement* – particularly in the light of McEwan's later attempts to oppose terror and literature through the idea of the moral imagination – are the remarkable *parallels* it throws up between the figures of the novelist and the terrorist. It is not just the banal truth that terrorists clearly possess an imagination, too, but that the novel is not quite the morally redemptive imaginative force it appears to be. As McEwan makes clear, it is by no means a coincidence that Briony's youthful melodrama *The Trials of Arabella* is 'intended to inspire not laughter, but terror, relief and instruction, in that order' (p. 8). On the contrary, the young girl's identification of Robbie as the 'principle of darkness' (p. 113) who threatens her very way of life is the result of nothing more insightful than her own melodramatic plot-driven imagination. In McEwan's account, it seems that the dangerously seductive power of story is its ability to fabricate, rather than merely reflect, the lives of others:

> Surely, it was not too childish to say that there had to be a story; and this was the story of a man whom everybody liked, but about whom the heroine always had her doubts, and finally she was able to reveal that he was the incarnation of evil. (p. 115)

For Briony, this childlike faith in the tale of 'terror, relief and instruction, in that order' leads her to commit the sin for which she will spend the rest of her life attempting to atone: she falsely accuses Robbie of raping her teenaged cousin Lola and he and Cecilia are separated forever. By the same token, the precise nature of her moral transgression will have an ironic resonance for McEwan's post-September 11 readership. Quite simply, the young Briony fails the same moral test of the imagination as Mohammed Atta: both are unable or unwilling to grasp the simple fact that other people are as real as them. Nor do the parallels stop there. Both, at least according to McEwan's accounts, mythologize themselves as quasi-religious saviours or protectors; both possess a utopian rage for order and symmetry; both are driven by a disgust and fascination for the messiness of the real; and both demonize their victims as the 'incarnation of evil'. If both know that they are right (p. 170), it is only because they prefer a dangerous certainty – an unreasonable belief or knowledge – to the ocular proof of empirical evidence. Perhaps Briony's account of giving false testimony against Robbie even offers a compelling psychological study of the self-radicalization of the novelist-as-fundamentalist: 'By clinging tightly to what she believed she knew, narrowing her thoughts, reiterating her testimony, she was able to keep from mind the damage she only dimly sensed she was doing' (p. 170).

For McEwan, moreover, *Atonement* is not simply a story about Briony but about the moral ambiguity of the novel more generally. It goes without saying that his heroine is a deeply flawed, self-deluding figure throughout – even she wonders whether she has changed all that much from her spoilt childhood self – but *Atonement* does not let her fellow storytellers off so lightly. To be sure, Briony remains a devastating study of the novelist-as-narcissist but the larger question McEwan raises is whether the novelistic 'moral imagination' might not itself be something of a contradiction-in-terms: does story really enable us to experience the lives of others as they are lived or, as Briony suspects, is it a way of turning them into little narrative machines with no existence independent of our own? From an ethical way of being in the world, we move to a darker idea of the novel as a kind of narrativized narcissism that expands to fill in the gaps where empathy should be. When she sends her first novella off to *Horizon* – in a form that dutifully recreates the encounter between Cecilia and Robbie from each perspective – Briony's manuscript is rejected on the grounds that – for all its modish Bergsonian explorations of consciousness – nothing really happens: 'Your most sophisticated readers . . . retain a childlike desire to be told a story, to be held in suspense, to know what happens' (p. 314). The story of other minds, each possessing equal value, is clearly not enough, even for such sophisticated readers as Elizabeth Bowen and Cyril Connolly. If there is a lesson to be learnt here, it is that Briony's childlike faith in the power of story was right all along (at least when it comes to writing books) and this desire to tell a story – as much as a readiness to set the record straight – is what dictates her fictional re-imaginings of the story of Robbie and Cecilia. In the famous coda to McEwan's novel – where the romantic reunion of the two lovers is revealed to be a purely fictional act of atonement by the woman who drove them apart in the first place – Briony justifies her rewriting of history by appealing once again to the inescapable narrative logic of terror, relief and instruction:

> I know there's always a certain kind of reader who will be com-pelled to ask, But what *really* happened? The answer is simple: the lovers survive and flourish. As long as there is a single copy, a solitary typescript of my final draft, then my spontaneous, for-tuitous sister and her medical prince survive to love. (p. 371)

Perhaps we might see this claim as final proof of Briony's boundless capacity for self-delusion but – for all the pitilessness of his own denouement – McEwan himself is not immune to the senti-mental force of such logic. It is certainly tempting to wonder whether the almost sadistic ingenuity of the novel's final, beautifully delayed, revelation – that Cecilia and Robbie did not live happily ever after, that they died young and miserably without ever reuniting – would have met with the precocious Briony's approval. After all, we still get terror, relief and instruction – albeit not quite in that order. The rhe-torical thrill of pulling rabbits out of hats (even dead ones) lingers on in a work that, officially at least, prefers the messiness of real life to cheap plot tricks. This may, however, be precisely what McEwan him-self is acknowledging: the childish desire to please and be pleased is what writing and reading novels, even this one, are all about. We are all Brionys.

## 4

In the larger context of his thought and work, we might see *Atonement* as a book that subjects McEwan's conviction about the novelist's moral imagination to a severe trial of faith: belief in the saving power of art is potentially just as infantile, solipsistic and dangerous as any other belief. It is striking, then, that this faith resurfaces in different form in his first post-9/11 novel *Saturday* (2005). At face value, of course, it would be difficult to find a character less like Briony Tallis than *Saturday*'s protagonist. Henry Perowne – a neuroscientist, a literary philistine with no patience for the loose and baggy monster that is the novel, a very English pragmatist who is distrustful of anything smacking of utopian grand narratives – sees himself as living proof that people *can* live without stories.[13] Yet, Henry, like Briony (and Joe Rose before her), is, if not exactly wrong, then at least reliably unreliable in his judgements; he, too, is unable to learn the lesson of the story in which he is a character, which, of course, is that stories are harder to live without than you might think. To be sure, Henry has never had the time or energy to read Darwin but he instinctively believes the New Atheist narrative of scientific progress and even jokes to his daughter that if he were asked to construct a religion it would be the religion of evolution:

> What better creation myth? An unimaginable sweep of time, numberless generations spawning by infinitesimal steps complex living beauty out of inert matter, driven on by the blind furies of random mutation, natural selection and environmental change, with the tragedy of forms continually dying, and lately the wonder of minds emerging and with them morality, love, art, cities – and the unprecedented bonus of this story happening to be demonstrably true. (*Saturday*, p. 56)

For Henry, moreover, it seems that there is no doubt who the guiding deity – the secular sky god – of this new creation myth should be: metropolitan man sits at the top of the evolutionary tree. '[I]f the presentation dispensation is wiped out now', he muses, 'the future will look back on us as gods, certainly in this city, lucky gods blessed by supermarket cornucopias, torrents of accessible information, warm clothes that weigh nothing, extended life-spans, wondrous machines' (p. 77). Perhaps McEwan's narrator is right to say that we are living in the best of all possible worlds – this is certainly true of his own tidy, contented one – but it is not difficult to detect a note of quiet bourgeois hubris here that invites nemesis in the queasy and fearful aftermath of 9/11. What if the 'present dispensation' *is* wiped out now?

For McEwan, of course, *Saturday* is his real 9/11 novel because it allegorically stages the war he saw being waged that day: literature versus terror, empathy against solipsism, 'harmless streets like these and the tolerant life they embody' faced with a 'new enemy – well-organised, tentacular, full of hatred and focused zeal' (*Saturday*, p. 76). On one side of this battle, we have Henry, and Henry, it seems, has everything: the successful job, the happy marriage, the Georgian terraced house in Fitzrovia and two eerily perfect kids in Blues prodigy Theo and Faber poetess Daisy. On the other, we have the tragi-comic thug Baxter, who has very little to start with and will soon have nothing at all: he suffers from a degenerative neurological condition and stands, more generally, for the ever-present threat of violence against the happy English home. However, the real difference here is that this conflict is not played out through the novel form but through other forms of art. To Henry – who performs brain surgery while listening to Bach and casually drops in on his son's Blues band's rehearsals – music represents the only kind of utopia it is still acceptable to believe in:

> Out in the real world there exist detailed plans, visionary projects for peaceable realms, all conflicts resolved, happiness for everyone, for ever – mirages for which people are prepared to die and kill. Christ's kingdom on earth, the workers' paradise, the ideal Islamic state. But only in music, and only on rare occasions, does the curtain actually lift on this dream of community, and it's tantalisingly conjured, before fading away with the last notes. (pp. 171–2)

What is the meaning of the particular riff on the 'End of the World Blues'? Just as the novel form allows us to occupy many different minds at once, so music, too, permits us to inhabit a kind of imagined community where, at least temporarily, self and other can coexist peacefully: the aesthetic experience is at one and the same time a moral one. If this musical utopia is explicitly anti-religious – the point being that it does not and can never exist in reality – Bach and the Blues are nonetheless interesting choices for an atheist's iPod. Perhaps Theo's Christian name is more than a coincidence here, for music recognizably fills a God-shaped hole, bringing peace, consolation and temporary redemption to a world that would otherwise be chaotic, arbitrary and meaningless. In Henry's resolutely story-free world, only music enables him to experience what his eminent father-in-law, the poet John Grammaticus, claims to find in Daisy's verse: 'secular transcendence' (p. 138).

The menacing 'real world' that threatens the contented Perowne family is, by contrast, always imagined at one remove, like the women in burkhas Henry sneers at from behind the windshield of his Mercedes S500 (p. 124). It is too crude to accuse McEwan of sharing the anti-Islamic prejudices of his hero: *Saturday* is, in many ways, a novel *about* prejudice, misunderstanding and over-interpretation in an increasingly paranoid London.[14] Even so, Henry does seem to have been dipping into at least some of his creator's post-9/11 bedtime reading. As we have already begun to see in our introduction, the New Atheist novelist's representation of what they call 'Islam' – and it is revealing that they do speak of such a monolithic entity – is little more than a mosaic of quotations from each other's works, from that of fellow travellers like Harris and Hitchens, and from neo-Orientalists like Bernard Lewis and Paul Berman. For McEwan, Islam in particular, and organized religion in general, is characterized by what he calls a 'troubled relationship with curiosity' ('End of the World Blues', p. 363): this is, of course, a not very euphemistic way of saying that it is insular and backward-looking. However, it has to be said that this 'insight' is not, in itself, a very ground-breaking one: Martin Amis makes exactly the same point in an essay called 'Terror and Boredom' (2002) and even he seems to have lifted it directly from a now rather dated thesis of Bernard Lewis.[15] One gets the same feeling of *déjà vu* throughout *Saturday* whenever Islam is mentioned. If Henry and Theo are as different as any father and teenage son, for instance, we still find them bonding over what seems, on the face of it, to be an unlikely respect for the work of Christopher Hitchens: why else would they speak of the 'self-pity' of Islam? (*Saturday*, p. 34).[16] While Daisy argues violently with her father over the merits of the Iraq invasion, she, too, shares Hitchens, Harris and Amis's contempt for the ultra-liberal or postmodern 'relativism' that has supposedly allowed Saddam Hussein's regime to prosper (p. 192). Perhaps it is no accident, either, that the only Muslim character Henry directly encounters – an Iraqi refugee who was tortured under Saddam – is the least imagined in the book: Miri Taleb exists only as a star witness for the prosecution in Henry's case for war (pp. 62–4).

Finally, we have the simian Baxter, whose irrational desire for vengeance after Henry accidentally prangs his car seems to embody the arbitrary threat of Islamist terror as a whole. It would have been incredibly crass, of course, to make Baxter himself an Islamist: *Saturday* prefers to stay within the confines of (clunky) allegory rather than risk turning into a Daily Mail-style rant. Yet, what we are dealing with here is, nonetheless, a difference of degree, not kind. As McEwan makes clear on many occasions from *Enduring Love* onwards, he sees a continuum between religious faith and neuro-pathology: 'It is not for nothing that one of the symptoms in a developing psychosis, noted and described by psychiatrists, is "religiosity"' ('End of the World Blues', p. 365). For Henry, moreover, religious believers suffer from what his psychiatric colleagues politely call an 'excess of the subjective':

> The primitive thinking of the supernaturally inclined amounts to what his colleagues call a problem, or an idea, of reference. An excess of the subjective, the ordering of the world in line with your needs, an inability to contemplate your own unimportance. In Henry's view, such reasoning belongs on a spectrum at whose far end, rearing like an abandoned temple, lies psychosis. (*Saturday*, p. 17)

If we believe in a supernatural deity at all, it seems that we are already on a road that leads to the psychotic solipsism of Mohammed Atta where other people simply cease to exist. We have already seen this pathology in *Enduring Love*'s Jed Parry and we can find it again in Baxter who watches the Stop the War marchers with '*a false sense of superiority* . . . somewhat short of, a little less disabling than, those other neurological conditions – grandiosity, delusions of grandeur' (p. 91). Perhaps more poignantly, McEwan also shows us how Baxter's fragile swagger is purchased by a blind faith in the possibility of being redeemed from his own personal neurological hell, if not by God, then at least by His modern equivalent, the doctor. In the aftermath of Henry's initial confrontation with Baxter, what saves Perowne from a savage beating is Baxter's even more savage belief that it is Perowne who can save *him*: 'They are together, he and Perowne, in a world, not of the medical, but of the magical. When you're diseased, it is unwise to abuse the shaman' (p. 95).

Perhaps the most famous (or notorious) instance of what we have called secular transcendence in McEwan's fiction is the climax to *Saturday* where the two worlds of Henry and Baxter finally crash head on. It is here, more than anywhere else in McEwan's work, that we encounter the mythopoeic dimension to his atheism and, characteristically, the vehicle for this myth is literature. After being humiliated by Henry following the car accident, Baxter, armed with a knife, breaks into the Perowne home where a family reunion is taking place. He demands that Daisy, the young poet, strip off her clothes and read him some of her verse, which he sees lying on the table. In a trembling but increasingly confident voice, the naked Daisy instead reads Mathew Arnold's 'Dover Beach' – which Baxter mistakes for one of her efforts – and the effect is a sudden change in the mood of her assailant:

> . . . Baxter has broken his silence and is saying excitedly, 'You wrote that. You *wrote* that.'
> It's a statement, not a question. Daisy stares at him, waiting.
> He says again, 'You wrote that.' And then, hurriedly, 'It's beautiful. You know that, don't you. It's beautiful. And you wrote it.' (p. 222)

To put it mildly, Baxter's transformation from potential rapist to poetry lover is unlikely – one is tempted to say miraculous – but in the context of McEwan's neo-Victorian faith in literature, empathy and the moral imagination it makes perfect sense. It is no coincidence, either, that what brings about this change in Baxter is 'Dover Beach' – a poem that finds consolation for lost religious faith in the private religion of human relation ('Ah, love, let us be true / To one another!'). Just as reading a few novels might have given Mohammed Atta pause for thought, so hearing a nice poem about relationships is enough to stop a rapist dead in his tracks. If it would be going too far to say that literature redeems Baxter – just to be on the safe side young Theo throws him down a flight of stairs – this 'lord of terror' is, at least temporarily, transformed into an 'amazed admirer' (p. 223) before the prospect of another existence: 'his smile is wet and beatific' and his voice 'trembles with exalted feeling' (p. 224). For the atheist McEwan, of course, what transports Baxter is not a recognition of the existence of God, but rather of the existence of another human being ('you wrote it'), who, in turn, reminds Baxter of the fragility of his own existence:

> Daisy recited a poem that cast a spell on one man. Perhaps any poem would have done the trick, and thrown the switch on a

sudden mood change. Still, Baxter fell for the magic, he was transfixed by it, and he was reminded how much he wanted to live. (p. 278)

So, what are we to make of the 'spell' with which *Saturday* concludes? It goes without saying that McEwan is too card-carrying a sceptic to fall for the magic of poetry himself, and the novel carefully hedges its bets. On the one hand, the Bach-loving Henry is characteristically tone-deaf to the lyrical music heard by Baxter: he, too, thinks Daisy wrote the poem, but he almost comically misreads its meaning. On the other, John Grammaticus is another study in the childish narcissism of the Great Writer: he is a male Briony Tallis with a drink problem. Lastly, of course, we have the narrative black hole of Baxter himself: was he moved so much by Daisy's poem that he fell in love with her (as Grammaticus believes) or (as Perowne prefers) was his reaction just one more violent mood-swing induced by faulty neurones? Yet, the bare fact that the novel permits the unlikely encounter between Arnold and Baxter – between literature and terror – to take place at all might be what is most revealing in this instance. To be sure, McEwan could easily be accused of pulling just one more rhetorical rabbit out of the hat here: what is ostensibly a novel about the sprawling, uncontrollable disorder of everyday life is, once again, filled with the clean lines, perfect symmetry and unlikely coincidences that are the fatal signs of its author's control-freakery. If the meeting between Daisy and Baxter stretches the novel's credibility to breaking point – and arguably beyond – the fact that McEwan allows it to happen anyway perhaps reveals that his own belief in the moral force of fiction may ultimately be beyond rationality as well: James Wood calls the novelist's belief in the redemptive force of art 'a hope, a flourish, a plangent asymmetry' ('On a Darkling Plain') but we might just as easily call it a faith. Perhaps we might even see the climax as an exercise in the magical realist fiction that Henry most detests, for what it depicts is precisely the kind of miraculous, impossible metamorphosis from devil to angel this no-nonsense neuroscientist finds so difficult to swallow: 'What were these authors of reputation doing – grown men and women of the twentieth century – granting supernatural powers to their characters?' (*Saturday*, p. 67). Such a question could easily be posed to the author of one of the magical realist books Henry has evidently tried to read: Ian McEwan himself.[17] For

McEwan – a full-grown, twentieth-century author of reputation – it seems as if *Saturday* is a fragile profession of faith in the supernatural power of literature itself, and the novel demands the same leap of faith from its readers in order to work its secular magic. In many ways, Henry's own Pascalian wager aptly describes the wager of *Saturday* as well:

> It doesn't sound plausible. But in general, the human disposition is to believe. And when proved wrong, shift ground. Or have faith, and go on believing. Over time, down through the generations, this may have been the most efficient: just in case, believe. (p. 151)

## 5

In 'End of the World Blues', McEwan gives a typically novelistic explanation for the peculiar fascination that the human race has with end-time thinking: 'we all have need of a plot, a narrative, to shore up our irrelevance in the face of things' (p. 357). It seems that, regardless of whether we believe in sky gods or not, we all have faith in the power of story to explain where we have come from and where we are going in a universe that would otherwise seem utterly random. As the essay goes on to speculate, and as this chapter has sought to show, what this means is that the struggle between religion and science will not ultimately turn upon the question of which is more true, but upon which offers a better narrative, a more compelling creation myth for its readers (p. 360). To our eyes, McEwan's plangent appeal to the power of art in *Saturday* is the high point of his faith in secularism's ability to out-narrate religion, but in many ways the recent novella *On Chesil Beach* (2007) – a black and white photograph of the post-Empire, pre-sexual liberation England of 1962 – represents a return to the sceptical prophecies of his earlier work.[18] Edward Mayhew, the budding scholar who is the novella's hero, sees religious visions of the end of the world as something that quite literally belong in the history books. He reads Norman Cohn's *Pursuit of the Millennium* – with its tragi-comic litany of deluded, would-be Messiahs – and is grateful 'to live in a time when religion had generally faded into insignificance' (*On Chesil Beach*, p. 45). Yet, even as Edward and his new bride Florence eat their wedding meal, the wireless brings news of a fresh wave of prophets of the end of days: Macmillan's winds of change, nuclear sabre-rattling over Berlin and even something called the World Islamic Conference in Baghdad. For Edward's mother-in-law, an Oxford philosophy don, the young man's modish left-wing politics – he is a Labour man, a member of CND and someone who feels a vague 'duty to help save the world' (p. 47) – are themselves merely the latest expression of the religious millenarianism he reads about in medieval history:

> What part did famine or social change have in providing followers? And with their anti-Semitism and attacks on the Church and the merchants, couldn't the movements be seen as an early form of socialism of the Russian type? And then, also provocatively, wasn't nuclear war the modern equivalent to the Apocalypse of the Book of Revelation, and were we not always bound by our history and our guilty nature to dream of our annihilation? (pp. 117–18)

Just like Bernard Tremaine, Joe Rose and Henry Perowne before him, then, Edward is what we might call a McEwan rationalist who commits the cardinal error of believing that he has no 'beliefs'. If he is too modest to mistake himself for one of Norman Cohn's deluded Messiahs, it is no accident that Edward, too, finds himself washed up on the beach of history: this naïve believer in the 'great man' school of historical change – 'was it really outmoded to believe that forceful individuals could change the course of history?' (p. 13) – finds his own life changed forever because at a crucial moment on Chesil Beach he did nothing for no good reason. Perhaps we might describe McEwan's novella as his own melancholy End of the World Blues, then, but with one crucial difference: what seem to be dying out here are not religious fantasies of world-purifying annihilation so much as the rational belief in progress towards perpetual peace. W(h)ither the socialist dream of peace, jobs and freedom in the epoch of ever-rising religious fundamentalism, September 11 and the War on Terror? In this sense, we might see *On Chesil Beach* as a kind of New Atheist rewriting of 'Dover Beach', in which a pair of perfectly rational lovers are confronted, not with the 'long withdrawing roar' of the Sea of Faith, but with its equally miserable return. The trouble with tides is that they tend to come back in again.

## CHAPTER TWO

# MARTIN AMIS AND THE WAR FOR CLICHÉ

Martin Amis – novelist, critic and lifelong non-believer – recently declared that he is now 'not quite' an atheist.[1] It would be premature, though, to say that he has undergone some kind of Damascene conversion. As he makes clear in 'The Voice of the Lonely Crowd' (2002), Amis remains a committed opponent of religion: 'Religious belief is without reason and without dignity, and its record is near-universally dreadful' (*The Second Plane*, p. 14). However, he goes on to add that atheism is *itself* a belief system that is not entirely borne out by what evidence we have. To put it in Amis's own succinct words, what lies on the other side of religion is not atheism, secularism or any other *ism*: 'it is independence of mind – that's all' (pp. 77–8). If he is not quite a card-carrying New Atheist, though, it is clear that Amis remains – ideologically and politically – something of a fellow-traveller: the novelist is a self-appointed champion of secular enlightenment values, a dedicated opponent of what he sees as the return of medieval monotheism and (like his friend Ian McEwan) an admirer of the work of Hitchens and Harris.[2] Just as the New Atheists supplant belief in a supernatural God with a reverence for nature, so Amis's own agnosticism comes close to being a cosmological piety: 'the universe is far more bizarre, prodigious and chillingly grand than any doctrine', he writes, and any 'spiritual needs can be met by its contemplation' (p. 15). Perhaps the single most revealing index of Amis's own secular piety is – just as we saw in the case of Ian McEwan – a belief in literature and particularly, the literary imagination. On the one side, the literary imagination is the embodiment of freedom, originality and what he calls 'independence of mind'. On the other, the religious mind is consistently depicted as impoverished, sheep-like and straitjacketed by centuries of tradition. For Amis, this

literary war against cliché is, as we will see, played out most fiercely –
and, needless to say, most controversially – in his writings on Islam
and 'Islamism'. What happens, then, when the heroically independent figure of the New Atheist novelist is pitted against 'The Voice of
the Lonely Crowd' that is religious, and more particularly, Islamic,
fundamentalism?

## 1

In 'The Voice of the Lonely Crowd', which has recently been republished in his controversial collection *The Second Plane* (2008),
Amis addresses the question of what – if any – purpose literature has
in the post-9/11 world. He quickly moves into a larger philosophical
debate about the purpose of literature in general. As McEwan notes
in 'End of the World Blues', the very desire to find a 'purpose' – an
overarching plot or narrative that gives meaning to human existence
in a universe that would otherwise be chaotic – is inextricably bound
up with literature and we can see something of the same argument in
Amis. We all require an 'assertion of human pride' – a humanistic
counterweight – in the face of the cold immensity of a universe without god (pp. 15–16). To Amis's own eyes, this human desire for dignity, value or meaning can take many different forms – James
Lovelock's Gaia theory is mooted, as is the pugnacious humanism of
Dawkins and Hitchens – but, like McEwan, the novelist ultimately
settles on the consolations of his own profession:

> a strategy with a rather longer history centres on an intensified
> reverence for art – or in Matthew Arnold's formula, for 'the best
> which has been thought and said'.
>     Literature – the aggregate of written works – has always been the
> most persistent candidate for cultification (p. 16).

Why is literature the most popular object for secular devotion? For
Amis – like McEwan again – the cult of the literary represents the
acceptable face of religion because, first of all, it worships a transcendental deity that actually exists: 'there is, after all, something
tangible to venerate – something boundless, beautiful, and divinely
bright' (p. 16). If literature is just about the only divinity in which it
is still possible to believe, though, what really attracts Amis is its
stubborn *resistance* to every historical attempt to turn it into object

of collective worship, an ideological tool or political weapon: the literary is almost by definition a cult of one. On the one hand, it resisted F. R. Leavis's attempts in the 1930s to impose upon it his own authoritarian value judgements in the name of an empty signifier called 'life'. On the other, it also evades the contemporary academy's attempts to disallow value judgements at all in the name of an equally vacuous 'political correctness' (pp. 17–19). Finally, and perhaps most importantly, though, literature always stands over and against religion:

> Literature forms a single body of thought, yet its voices are intransigently and unenlargeably individual. And the voice of religion, to reposition a phrase often used by that great critic, the Reverend Northrop Frye, is 'the voice of the lonely crowd'. It is a monologue that seeks the validation of a chorus. (p. 16)

To Amis's way of thinking, then, literature is the voice of singularity, independence of mind and 'the ideology of *no* ideology' (p. 19). Its moral purpose does not so much lie in its ability to inhabit the lives of others – as Ian McEwan would have it – but rather in enabling us to write and think like no one but ourselves. As he shows in the foreword to an earlier anthology of his essays and reviews, this relentlessly individualizing quality is also why the voice of literature wages war against the cliché:

> To idealise: all writing is a campaign against cliché. Not just clichés of the pen but clichés of the mind and clichés of the heart. When I dispraise, I am usually quoting clichés. When I praise, I am usually quoting the opposed qualities of freshness, energy and reverberation of voice.[3]

For Amis, it is clear that his own personal war against cliché is not simply the caprice of a Nabokovian prose stylist so much as the linguistic front of a moral and political struggle: 'style', he writes in an essay on Saul Bellow, 'is morality. Style judges' (*The War Against Cliché*, p. 467). To resort to a cliché, a stock formulation or habitual response, he argues, is to pass up an opportunity to think or feel for oneself. Perhaps this is why, in another review, Amis attributes Philip Larkin's casual racism to nothing more sinister than laziness: 'Like mood-clichés, Larkin's racist snarls were inherited propositions, shamefully unexamined, humiliatingly average' (p. 164). If Larkin remains the prisoner of the 'humiliatingly' average – with devastating results for his reputation – Joyce's *Ulysses* is, by contrast, a one-man war against the cliché-mongers of Catholic nationalist Ireland:

> *Ulysses* is *about* cliché. It is about inherited, ready-made formulations, fossilised metaphors – most notably those of Irish Catholicism and anti-semitism. After all, prejudices are clichés: they are secondhand hatreds. (p. 444)

In retrospect, we can already see Amis laying the groundwork for his own stylistic version of the New Atheist novel here. On the one side, we have literature and, with it, individuality, originality and freedom of expression. On the other, we have cliché, prejudice, racism, anti-Semitism, Catholicism and, just around the corner, a new and even more dangerous enemy. What better target could there be for the war against cliché, after all, than the misogynist, anti-Semitic dogma of radical Islamism?

So what, before we go any further, are we to make of Amis's attempt to pit literature against religion? It is not, on the face of it, much more convincing than Ian McEwan's desire to champion the literary imagination over and against the forces of terror. Once again, we can detect an element of *bellelettrist* wish-fulfilment in this fusion of style and morality – as if freedom from prejudice, error and so on were simply a matter of finding *le mot juste*. However there is also something historically wrong-headed about such a transparent attempt to de-convert literature. To put it bluntly, Amis is guilty of the very charge he levels against Leavis and the PC Brigade: he posits his own narrow historical idea of literary value – which is broadly high modernist in origin – as a timeless, a-historical definition of 'literature' as such.[4] One can't help but wonder what some of the writers he cites and admires – Frye, Arnold, not to mention Eliot or Donne or Milton or Dante – would make of the attempt to oppose literary expression to religious belief. While Amis's somewhat Oedipal animus towards F. R. Leavis is ever-present in his criticism, his Olympian tone remains recognizably Leavisite: the literary critic's job is still to judge, literary judgements are still moral judgements and the Great Tradition still exists, even if its centre of gravity has shifted westwards from England to the East Coast of the USA.[5] For us, though, the most dangerous upshot of Amis's historical naiveté –

his belief that he is not being 'historical' at all – is the assumption that his description of the literary is not political or ideological either. Reading Amis claiming that the writer espouses freedom, individuality and 'no ideology', for instance, we are reminded of Paul Ricoeur's argument that this is in fact the ideological claim *par excellence*: 'for it is always the other who stoops to ideology'.[6] If the war against cliché is harmless enough when its principal target is merely the baroque pulp of Thomas Harris (pp. 233–41), it becomes more problematic when, as we will see, the target switches to Islam: Amis's struggle between literature and religion – reason versus unreason, freedom versus slavery, secular enlightenment versus *odium theologicum* – comes uncomfortably close to Samuel Huntington's 'clash of civilisations'.[7] On the one side, it is striking that *The War against Cliché*'s celebration of literature seems (with the honourable exception of Nabokov) to consist almost exclusively of paeans to the same Anglo-American authors: Bellow, Updike, Bellow, Roth, Bellow. On the other, we can't help but note that the Middle East's impact on literature seems to have been less positive: the only mention of Arabs in the entire book is to blame the 1973 OPEC oil embargo for the stagflation that brought the golden age of amateur, shoestring literary criticism to an end (pp. xii, 116). Perhaps more controversially, what we might be tempted to call Amis's literary neo-conservatism – Ziauddin Sardar coins the term 'Blitcon' to describe his work and that of McEwan and Rushdie[8] – also risks underestimating the aesthetic contribution of one particular 'oil-state' Arab: Saudi-born Osama Bin Laden. Just as McEwan's attempt to pit the literary imagination against the solipsism of terrorism smacked of wishful thinking, so Amis's own effort to oppose literary individuality to the herd instinct of the religious seems equally self-aggrandizing: September 11 was a great many things but it certainly wasn't a cliché. In Amis's post-9/11 literature, the New Atheist novel confronts – not the second-hand currencies of religious belief – but a new and formidable warrior-against-cliché.

## 2

In 'The Voice of the Lonely Crowd', Amis describes his discomfort at remembering on September 11 that he was the author of a new book called *The War against Cliché*. 'Actually', he concedes, 'we can live with cliché. What we have to do now, more testingly, is live with war'

(*The Second Plane*, p. 13). Yet, we soon get the sense that it is cliché, actually, that the novelist can't live with after all: style is morality, remember, and the politics of language is one of the central themes of *The Second Plane*. To begin with, Amis sees Islamism as itself a kind of global war *for* cliché:

> The champions of militant Islam are, of course, misogynists, woman-haters; they are also misologists – haters of reason. Their armed doctrine is little more than a chaotic penal code underscored by impotent dreams of genocide. And, like all religions, it is a massive agglutination of stock response, of clichés, of inherited and unexamined formulations. This is the thrust of one of the greatest novels ever written, *Ulysses*, in which Joyce identifies Roman Catholicism, and anti-Semitism, as fossilisations of dead prose and dead thought. (p. 19)

For the fastidious stylist Amis, what appals most about everything from Sayyid Qutb's *Milestones* to the collected speeches of Osama Bin Laden is not so much the hate-filled ideology but the imaginative and intellectual poverty of the prose. We learn of the 'leaden-witted circularity' of Qutb (p. 61), the 'classic circularity' of Shia eschatology (p. 126) and – in case we haven't got the point yet – the 'circular gullibility' of al-Qaeda (p. 147). If Islamism's language is a closed feedback loop, then so must be the Islamist psyche and this brings us to the main thesis of Amis's writings on September 11: the Islamist mind is 'dependent' – inert, vacant, airless – and thus utterly impermeable to our logic, reason or understanding. Just as the perfect vacuum of Sayyid Qutb comes to embody the dependent mind, so another figure comes quite naturally to fill the role of the independent one: the resolutely individual writer. Perhaps appropriately, *The Second Plane* concludes with a stirring appeal to resist letting the name 'September 11' itself degenerate to the level of cliché, stock response or unexamined formulation lest the event it names should lose its singular force: 'let's call it by its proper name; let's not suggest that our experience of that event, that development, has been frictionlessly absorbed and filed away' (p. 206).

To our eyes, it is this last claim that represents the litmus test of *The Second Plane*: has Amis really saved the name of September 11 or does his own feline prose also manage to finesse it away? As Marjorie Perloff has pointed out, the problem with Amis's one-man war against the clichés of Islam is how quickly (despite its author's initial scepticism about the invasion of Iraq) it morphs into a set of clichés for war.[9] It is not just point-scoring – given that Amis is the one who sets the high modernist rules – to note the 'agglutination' of stock responses in his own prose: this is a book in which (to open a few pages at random) people are 'playing for time' (p. 12); night is 'closing in' (p. 47); events should have 'given us pause' (p. 85) and things, more likely than not, will 'come to pass' (p. 85). Yet, as the novelist himself tells us, style is never just an aesthetic adornment to content and the second-hand nature of the prose betrays a similar derivativeness at the level of ideas, particularly where Islam is concerned. Quite simply, *The Second Plane* is as much a book about other books as *The War against Cliché*: we encounter only one real live Muslim in the entire text and this is an over-zealous gatekeeper at the Dome of the Rock in Jerusalem to whom the novelist a little paranoidly ascribes a murderous intent (p. 91). For Amis, Islamic culture is chiefly characterized by an 'extreme incuriosity' about the outside world (p. 79) but – like Ian McEwan, who coincidentally accuses Islam of a 'troubled relationship with curiosity' in 'End of the World Blues' – the author himself is scarcely immune to his own charge. Both writers borrow almost all their insights from the same very small rock pool of sources: the F. R. Leavis of Orientalism, Bernard Lewis, the muscular liberal Paul Berman, the hard-right ideologue Mark Steyn and, of course, cronies like Hitchens and Harris. While Amis is ostentatiously respectful of the Prophet Mohammed himself – 'a revolutionary, a warrior, and a sovereign' is his curiously *Boy's Own Paper*-style assessment (pp. 49–50) – the novelist's account of the Muslim religion itself amounts to little more than a checklist of Neo-Conservative Orientalism: Islam is retrogressive (Lewis); irrational (Harris); a nihilist death cult (Berman and Harris) and, perhaps most importantly of all, a lethal cocktail of self-righteousness, self-pity and self-hatred (Hitchens). From the collapse of the Ottoman Empire, through the establishment of the state of Israel to the fiasco of the Six-Day War, the last century of Islamic history has been the story of a burning theological, political and even personal humiliation (pp. 79–82, 204–6). If the events of September 11 smack of a revival, they are in fact quite the opposite: what Amis calls 'Islamism' is in fact nothing more than the death drive of imperial Islam (p. 81). Perhaps it is this all-pervading sense of personal and political impotence that leads Amis to the closest

*The Second Plane* has to an original argument, if not, unfortunately, a particularly compelling one: Islamist terror is the product, not of anything so complex as theological history or international geopolitics, but male sexual frustration (pp. 47, 60, 67, 89). The historical impact of European colonialism, American interventionism and Israel's occupation of Palestine are as naught in comparison to the invasion of 'the last sanctum of male power' that is Islam (p. 89). This explosion of religious violence has its origins in the hormones rather than the head: it is a testosterone revolution. In *The Second Plane*, thus, the proper name of September 11 'with all its mystery, its instability, its terrible dynamism' (p. 206) finally turns out to be an Islamist brand of Viagra.

What exactly does Amis *mean* by 'Islamism' though? It is certainly odd that someone so alert to the politics of nominalism – 'September 11', 'The Axis of Evil', 'terrorism' – should deploy this charged noun without really troubling to define it. As we will see, this failure of definition lies at the heart of the accusations of Islamophobia levelled against the author by Terry Eagleton, following a notorious newspaper interview in which Amis expressed an 'urge' to exact a collective punishment on the Muslim community in Britain for the acts of a tiny extremist minority.[10] To be sure, Amis does consistently distinguish between Islam and Islamism in his published work even if the difference does not reflect particularly well on either:

> Millennial Islamism is an ideology superimposed upon a religion – illusion upon illusion. It is not merely violent in tendency. Violence is all that is there. (p. 91)

So, is Amis an Islamophobe? No: 'What I am is an Islamismophobe, or better say an anti-Islamist, because a phobia is an irrational fear, and it is not irrational to fear something that says it wants to kill you' (p. x).[11] However, the problem is that, even if we accept his own exceptionally fine distinction between Islam and Islamism, Amis himself continually blurs it. On the one hand, he does consistently use 'Islamism' to describe the politicization of Islam by such figures as Iqbal, Qutb, Khomeini and, more precisely, the murderous *Jihad*-ists of September 11: 'we respect Islam . . . [b]ut we do not respect Islamism', he portentously declares, 'just as we respect Mohammed and do not respect Mohammed Atta' (p. 50). On the other, though, 'Islamism' also seems to encompass not simply al-Qaeda, but Hamas,

Hizbullah, the Muslim Brotherhood in Egypt, the Algerian army (who in fact violently suppressed the Islamist *Front Islamique Salut*), the 'shoving, jabbing, jeering' young men of Peshawar who confront his friend Hitchens and, finally, the public face of all Islam everywhere: 'Islamism, as a mover and shaper of world events, is pretty well all there is' (p. 50).[12] Finally, in his depressingly positive review of a book by Mark Steyn, he gives up on the Islam/Islamist distinction altogether and boils everything down to a simple demographic numbers game: 'they' are out-breeding 'us' and 'we' need to get our act together (p. 157).[13] Perhaps it is not just coincidence that *The Second Plane* is dedicated to Amis's five children.

## 3

In our view, however, Amis's attempt to politicize the war against cliché rebounds on him in an even more disturbing sense: Islamist terror is not just a closed loop of endlessly circulating clichés but a new, horrifying and essentially creative rhetorical force. It is ironic, to start with, that his definition of 'literature' – independent, free-thinking, original in thought and expression – corresponds exactly to what the French literary critic Jean Paulhan once called periods of 'Terror'. According to Paulhan, 'Terror' describes ' those moments in the history of nations . . . when it suddenly seems that the State requires . . . an extreme purity of the soul, and the freshness of a communal innocence'.[14] For Paulhan, moreover, what distinguishes the terroristic pursuit of purity in its linguistic form is precisely an Amis-style war against cliché. Just like James Joyce ripping up the whole of literary history in *Ulysses*, the terrorist rhetorician reacts against the eighteenth-century over-codification of language into rhetoric, genre and other systems in the name of originality of expression, endless invention and renewal. If Paulhan raises the possibility that the novelist is closer to the terrorist than we might think, though, what is more interesting in Amis's writings on September 11 is the other side of that question. To what extent might the terrorist be a kind of novelist?

To be sure, Amis – like McEwan and, of course, Don DeLillo before him – draws a series of intriguing Dostoyevskian parallels between the aesthetic and the terrorist psyche beneath all the posturing about independent and dependent minds, reason and unreason. Both the novelist and the terrorist, for instance, originally operate in a reason-free zone: the aesthetic process is 'very mysterious', Amis writes, and a great deal of its work gets done 'beneath the threshold of consciousness' and 'without the intercession of reason' (p. 12). However, it seems at first that the analogy only stretches up to a point. For Amis, at least, the novel is ultimately a rational undertaking because its purpose is not the denial of 'the thing which is called World' (Ayatollah Khomeini) but the creation of new, alternative or parallel worlds with their own internal logic and reason:

> Imaginative writing is understood to be slightly mysterious. In fact it is very mysterious. A great deal of the work gets done beneath the threshold of consciousness, and without the intercession of reason. When the novelists went into newsprint about September 11, there was a murmur to the effect that they were now being obliged to snap out of their solipsistic daydreams: to attend, as best they could, to the facts of life. For politics – once defined as 'what's going on' – suddenly filled the sky. True, novelists don't normally write about what's going on; they write about what's not going on. Yet, the worlds so created aspire to pattern and shape and moral point. A novel is a rational undertaking; it is reason at play, perhaps, but it is still reason. (pp. 12–13)

Nevertheless, Amis himself recognizes that the thing about September 11 was that 'what's not going on' was precisely what *was* going on: the attacks were not simply one more fact of everyday life but 'the worldflash of a coming future' (p. 3). Quite simply, what filled the sky that day according to this logic was not just politics but the *novel*: the irruption of a symbolic new world into the old one. Perhaps the most disturbing parallel between Amis's version of the novelist and the terrorist, though, is that the creative act both perform is intimately tied up with death, murder and more precisely, *suicide*. If any one thing explains Islamist terror for Amis – given his total lack of interest in seeking a political or even a theological rationale – it is that it is a pathological cult of mass death: the Islamist mind is a 'death-filled bog' (p. 147), it is 'crazed with blood and death' (p. 142) or, more prosaically, it is just plain 'abnormally interested in violence and death' (p. 201). Now, even if we put to one side the awkward fact that the author of books about the Holocaust (*Time's Arrow*), the Stalinist purges (*Koba the Dread, House of Meetings*), nuclear warfare (*Einstein's Monsters*) and September 11 (*The Second*

*Plane*) could hardly be said to be *normally* interested in violence and death,[15] it has to be said that Amis remains a curious case study of the artist-as-necrophiliac. Just as the Islamists see death as 'creative', a 'consummation' and 'a beginning' (p. 80), so his descriptions of the novel, too, depict it as a kind of necro-aesthetics living among and feeding off death, murder, even self-murder. From the war against 'the fossilisations of dead prose and dead thought' (p. 19), through the sudden and inexplicable loss of inspiration that renders a piece of fiction 'dead' ('as if your subconscious . . . has been neutralised or switched off') to the deliberate destruction or abandonment of 'not a dead thing, but a thriving novella', the creative process is itself a sacrificial cult that – in a way uncannily reminiscent of its terrorist other – creates new life against, with and sometimes through the material of mass death. In Norman Mailer's words, approvingly cited by Amis, 'one of the few real sorrows of the "spooky art" is that it requires you to spend too many days among dead things' (p. 51).

For Amis, moreover, it sometimes seems as if Bin Laden is the spooky artist *par excellence*. One of the more surprising aspects of *The Second Plane* is that – for all his disgust at the cliché-ridden, circular and dependent Islamist mind – Amis has a kind of appalled respect for the astonishing *coup de theatre* that was September 11. It was, he writes, an act of 'atrocious ingenuity' (p. 3), 'a desolating spectacle' (p. 6) with the 'capacity to astonish' (p. 9), something 'unbelievably radical' (p. 22), even a paradigm-shift (p. 53). As we saw in Chapter One, McEwan somewhat unimaginatively depicts the attacks as a failure of moral imagination – the act of people who could never step far enough outside of their own closed world view to put themselves in the position of their victims. Yet, Amis recognized straightaway that the attacks were, in fact, a considerable imaginative feat, an atrocity exhibition explicitly choreographed to reach the widest possible audience: 'such a *mise-en-scène* would have embarrassed a studio executive's storyboard or a thriller writer's notebook' (p. 4). To Amis's way of thinking, the literal and metaphorical architect of September 11 – Osama Bin Laden – is no mere Hollywood hack peddling clichés but a kind of neo-modernist conceptual artist delivering up the shock of the new:

> He must have anticipated that one or both of the towers would collapse. But no visionary cinematic genius could hope to recreate the majestic abjection of that double surrender, with the scale of

the buildings conferring its own slow motion. It was well understood that an edifice so demonstrably comprised of concrete and
steel would also become an unforgettable metaphor. This moment
was the apotheosis of the postmodern era – the era of images and
perceptions. (pp. 4–5)

Just as Henry Perowne notices that planes look different these
days – 'predatory or doomed' (*Saturday*, p. 16) – so Amis recognizes
that September 11 constituted a horrifying de-familiarization,
(*ostraneniye*, more literally, 'estrangement') of the world analogous
to what Viktor Shklovsky describes as the condition of 'literariness':
who, before that day, realized that a Boeing 747 was also a guided
missile? What is more, this art attack was conceived and executed on
a purely formal, symbolic level: the thing being de-familiarized and
re-appropriated here is not the real as such but the American imaginary. From the choice of weapon ('an American passenger jet is also
a symbol of indigenous mobility and zest' (*The Second Plane*, p. 6)),
through the symbolic rather than strategic targets (the WTC as
opposed to, say, a nuclear power station), all the way up to the 'unforgettable metaphor' of the collapsing towers, the September 11 attacks
fuse together the *objets trouvés* of America into a new and gigantic
work of militant political art:

> The bringers of Tuesday's terror were morally 'barbaric', inexpia-
> bly so, but they brought a demented sophistication to their work.
> They took these great American artefacts and pestled them
> together. (p. 6)[16]

In *The Second Plane*, Amis offers a refreshingly candid account of
just how dismal it felt to be a novelist getting back to work on the
morning of 12 September 2001: 'the so-called work in progress had
been reduced, overnight, to a blue streak of autistic babble' (p. 12).
Perhaps this is true, but the question lingers – reduced by what? The
tempting, if ungenerous, answer is by an attack of status anxiety.
There is a sense in which Amis and his peers were not overtaken by
the arrival of something called 'real life' – suddenly crashing into the
novelist's study like a plane into a skyscraper – but rather by the
hyper-novelization of life itself by a new warrior-against-cliché.
This new version of Paulhan's terrorist rhetorician relegates the
writer to the unaccustomed and dispiriting position of a *reader* of

someone else's fiction, or worse still, to that of a plodding literary critic, redundantly pointing out a powerful symbol here, an unforgettable metaphor there. Such is the fate of the terminally out-spooked artist.

So, what happens, then, when Amis is confronted with Bin Laden's horrifyingly effective version of the New Theist novel? It seems, at face value, that al-Qaeda's necro-aesthetics could not be further away from the aesthetics of secular transcendence, empathy and individuality valorized by the New Atheists: Bin Laden's inexpiable religious art redeems no one and nothing. At the same time, though, nothing is quite what it seems because, in one striking passage, Amis is willing to concede that the pathological death cult that is al-Qaeda possess not simply an imagination but a *moral* imagination and a moral purpose. In a striking re-imagining of the events leading up to September 11, the novelist puts the following rationale for the attacks into the mouth of the so-called 'American Taliban' John Walker Lindh:

> Now would be a good time to strike, John would tell Osama, because the West is enfeebled, not just by sex and alcohol, but also by thirty years of multicultural relativism. They'll think suicide-bombing is just an exotic foible, like shame-and-honour killings or female circumcision. Besides, it's religious, and they're always slow to question anything that calls itself that . . . And you'll be amazed by how long the word 'Islamophobia', as an unanswerable indictment, will cover Islamism too . . . Even if the Planes Operation succeeds, and thousands die, the Left will yawn and wonder why we waited so long. Strike now. Whatever we do, the liberals will all be saying that the West had it coming. Their ideology will make them reluctant to see what it is they confront. And it will make them slow learners. (pp. 72–3)

To be sure, Amis's terrorist ventriloquism can be seen as just one more act in a career-long attempt to *épater les bourgeois*: any liberal sneering at the neo-Orientalism of *The Second Plane* is, we are piously lectured, merely softening the ground for the third and the fourth planes. However, the fact remains that this argument *does* have an impeccably Orientalist – and thus wholly clichéd – pedigree: namely, the Christian tradition of seeing the rise of Islam as a precursor to the Day of Judgement. From Medieval writers fearful of the coming of the Moors to Martin Luther reflecting on the unconvertibility of the Turks, the rise of Islam is continually depicted throughout the Middle Ages as a divine judgement upon Christendom itself: it is a sign of the end of the age.[17] Such is the venerable religious tradition to which *The Second Plane* unwittingly belongs: where Luther conjured up the prospect of an army of unconvertible Turks at the gates of Vienna, so Amis imagines a horde of unredeemable Islamists checking in at Islamabad International Airport. Both Luther and Amis believe that we are just wasting our breath trying to reason with such people: we share no discourse, no conversation, no common values whatsoever with Islamists (p. x). Even more revealingly, Amis, too, sees the rise of Islamism as a harbinger of the imminent self-destruction of the decadent, morally bankrupt, West. For Amis, John Walker Lindh is *right* in his diagnosis of the 'enfeebled' West: 'we' *are* weak, naïve in our presumption of the rationality of our enemy (p. 70) and hamstrung by a doctrine of moral equivalence that sees no difference between Bin Laden and Bush (p. 200). Just as Luther sees the arrival of the Turks as the sign as a divine judgement upon the West, so Amis invokes the end-time vision of Yeats's *Second Coming*: 'the best lack all conviction, while the worst are full of passionate intensity' (p. 74). While insisting that Bin Laden committed 'a serious miscalculation' (p. 72) in believing the USA would be a soft target (but aren't Islamists supposed to be incapable of calculation?), Amis finds it difficult to control a sneaking suspicion that the Sheikh may have got it right after all. If we do not exactly 'have it coming' – as his parody of a bleeding heart liberal puts it – it may only be because we are already doing 'it' to ourselves: Western civilization, rendered increasingly infertile by our culture of rights and entitlements according to Mark Steyn (p. 159), is quite literally relativizing itself to death. Perhaps even Amis is not immune to a dose of what Ian McEwan calls the End of the World Blues: *The Second Plane* – that worldflash of a coming future – is a deeply retrogressive prophecy of the end of days.[18]

### 4

In a very literal sense, Amis's own New Atheist novel has yet to be written: he has published just one major work of fiction – 2003's badly received *Yellow Dog* – and two, equally criticized, short stories – 'In the Palace of the End' (2004) and 'The Last Days of Mohammed Atta' (2006) – that directly or even indirectly concern themselves with the events of September 11. A longer novella entitled 'The Unknown Known' was apparently abandoned by Amis himself. It could be argued, of course, that this reluctance to jump on the 9/11 literary bandwagon is entirely to his credit. As he rightly puts it in a 2004 interview to support *Yellow Dog*, 'it will be a while before any-one can really assimilate [9/11] and write a novel that doesn't look as though it's just blurted out'.[19] Yet, blurting or no blurting, the continuing absence of a Martin Amis novel about September 11, or Islamism, or terrorism does begin to look somewhat conspicuous from a writer who so loudly trumpets the values of literature over terror. For us, it often seems as if Amis is better at *writing about* September 11 – writing about what such writing will be like, or might be like, or would have been like if he had not already abandoned it – than producing his own fictional response. If the novelist is happy proselytizing for the far-reaching powers of the novel in his non-fiction writings, we have already begun to detect an anxiety throughout *The Second Plane* that the novelist's tradi-tional role as unacknowledged legislator of the world (*The Second Plane*, p. 16) has been usurped: the definitive 9/11 novel may already have been written, and on 9/11 itself. Perhaps Amis's sense of being condemned to play a futile game of catch-up is why he identifies, not himself, but Don DeLillo as the ideal candidate to write the definitive 9/11 work: 'he said, I think in *Mao II*, which is quite a way back, "The mood of the future is not going to be determined by writers; it's going to be determined by terrorists." And by Christ, they created a mood' ('Old Martin Amis Is in Your Face Again').[20] What, then, is the mood of Amis's own post-9/11 fiction?

For Amis, the 'blue streak of autistic babble' to which he was forced to return on the day after September 11 became the novel *Yellow Dog* (2003).[21] Its tone is, revealingly, the tone of all his post-9/11 fiction: an awkward mix of black comedy and treacly pathos. According to the novelist, this return to the comic genre – rather than, say, the portentous allegory of McEwan's *Saturday* – was a deliberate response to the prevailing atmosphere of the time. What seems at first glance to be a pale retread of former glories like *Money* (1984) is in fact a stoic assertion of business-as-usual in a new and terrifying age.[22] To Amis himself, *Yellow Dog* is a novel 'about what it feels like to be living in our current era, which established itself on September 11'[23] and – while it does not address those events directly – it is clearly saturated with a post-9/11 atmosphere:

> He stopped and thought: that feeling again. And he sniffed the essential wrongness of the air, with its fucked-up undertaste, as if all the sequiturs had been vacuumed out of it. A yellowworld of faith and fear, and paltry ingenuity. And all of us just flying blind. (*Yellow Dog*, p. 10)

What are the signs and wonders of this essential wrongness? From the casual act of GBH inflicted upon his hero Xan Meo in the opening pages, through random Islamist suicide bombings in London, to the imminent crash landing of a transatlantic jet, *Yellow Dog*'s frenetic action nominally concerns the 'obscenification of everyday life' (*Yellow Dog*, pp. 11, 335). Perhaps, though, it could just as easily be described as being about the banalization – the becoming-cliché – of terror. On the one hand, Neanderthal footballer Ainsley Car has already reduced unspeakable horror to the mindless hyperbole of sports commentary: 'I've put Hugalu on his arse, nutmegged Straganza, and laid it off for Martin Arris! The Twin Towers [of the original Wembley stadium – AB and AT] explode! With love, mate, with love!' (p. 49). On the other, Princess Victoria, teenage heiress to the British throne, decides that the only way in which she can avoid her Royal fate is by threatening to convert to Islam: 'I want to be a part of the *umma*' (p. 323). In the tragic-comic figure of Clint Smoker, a socially and sexually inadequate porn addict whose impotence ultimately drives him to murderous vengeance against the world, we even encounter a home-grown member of that prehominid species more usually found in Islamic countries: *homo Amis*.

Finally, we have the novel's protagonist, Xan Meo, whose own moral crash lies at the heart of *Yellow Dog*. After a vicious assault by an underworld boss which leaves him brain-damaged, Xan regresses into a psycho-sexual state of nature: this erstwhile model husband and father degenerates into a priapic caveman who tries to rape his wife and fixates upon his 4-year-old daughter. Yet, his neurological reverse engineering will already sound very familiar to readers of

Amis's writings on Islam because it is strangely akin to the novelist's depiction of the experience of radicalization. To Amis's way of thinking, September 11 was a day of 'De-Enlightenment' – 'a veritable Walpurgis night of the irrational' (*The Second Plane*, p. 13) and exactly the same description is applied to Xan's condition (*Yellow Dog*, p. 252). Both the head trauma victim and the Islamist convert exist in a testosterone-fuelled frenzy of rage, desire and frustration; both experience a sense of radical disconnect from 'the thing which is called world' (p. 97) and both transform that alienation into a thirst for violent revenge against women (p. 140). For Xan himself, his degeneration represents nothing less than a profession of faith – a *Shahāda* no less – in the religion of pure masculinity:

> . . . he felt that some historic wrong had at last found redress, as if his god, so inexplicably crippled, was once again more powerful than the god of his enemies. (p. 140)

Who else, the casual reader may wonder, believes that there is no god but God, *Lā ilaha illa al-Lāh*? While Amis is not so clumsy as to actually turn Xan into an Islamist convert, it is clear that he occupies the same neuro-chemical territory as the likes of Sayyid Qutb: both are the site of 'a collision . . . between a brain and a cat's cradle of glands' (*The Second Plane*, p. 91). Just like McEwan's *Saturday* – which offers a similar brew of religion, violence and neurology – *Yellow Dog* concludes by taking an unashamed refuge in the redeeming comforts of home, family, and once again, the novel: Xan manages to re-enlighten himself through reading, and finally writing, that most characteristically eighteenth century of literary modes, the sentimental letter (*Yellow Dog*, pp. 207–10, 306–8). If this is as close as Amis comes to the secular piety of the New Atheist novel – besides the occasional obligatory reference to Philip Larkin's 'Aubade' (*The Second Plane*, p. 91) – it has to be said that there is still something almost sanctimonious about a conclusion that feels it necessary to remind us, for instance, that newborn babies are very small.[24] The book is, fatally, much more at home imagining the 'yellow world of faith and fear' – epitomized by endless tedious riffs about the porn industry – than it ever is in this cosy domestic interior. This is a novelist who, it seems, shares much more of the Islamist's disgust, fascination and secret delight in what Khomeini calls the 'scum of existence' (*The Second Plane*, p. 80), in that unredeemable thing which is called 'world', than he likes to think. In one particularly unpleasant scene in the middle of *Yellow Dog* – curiously unmentioned in the yards of newsprint published after the Amis/Eagleton spat – a set of tabloid hacks respond to an Islamist suicide bombing in London by setting out a tough new editorial line on racial profiling: 'Anyone who looks remotely Arab should have their lives made an absolute torment for the rest of the century' (p. 161). Such passages are presumably Amis's idea of satire, but this makes it all the more dispiriting to find the author expressing a very similar (though supposedly spur-of-the-moment) urge three years later in his notorious *Times* interview: 'There's a definite urge – don't you have it? – to say, "The Muslim community will have to suffer until it gets its house in order".' Perhaps not even Amis is immune to the obscenification of everyday life.

## 5

In Martin Amis's one-man war against cliché, then, one is tempted to conclude that cliché is winning: the post-9/11 world poses an imaginative challenge that his fiction has not (at least not yet) risen to meet. It is terrorism's ability to out-imagine the novel that perhaps explains the desperate uncertainty of tone that plagues *Yellow Dog* and the three shorter fictions – two published, one abandoned – on 9/11 itself: Amis seems unable to decide whether to pass judgement upon the terrorists or, imaginatively at least, to become one. Even his default position of high ironic cool starts to sound like someone whistling in the dark to keep his spirits up. At any rate, the abandoned novella 'The Unknown Known' is a satire about Ayed, a 'diminutive Islamist terrorist' (*The Second Plane*, p. 52) who hatches a plot to unleash every compulsive rapist in the USA on the town of Greeley, Colorado (once briefly home to Sayyid Qutb); 'In the Palace of the End' is a blackly absurdist tale of a double hired to impersonate the son of a Saddam-style dictator and 'The Last Days of Mohammed Atta' imagines the hijacker as existing in a kind of Sartrean hell of endless existence. To be sure, Amis's familiar themes are present in all three stories: Islam is once again depicted as a peculiarly male cocktail of irrationality, sexual inadequacy and (in Atta's case) total nihilism. From the diminutive, ill-endowed Ayed, through the impotent son of the tyrant Saddam, to the horribly constipated Atta ('who has not moved his bowels since May'), the Islamist male is tormented throughout by a Bakhtinian grotesque body that mocks his pretensions to absolute power (p. 97). However, it has to be said that a certain sense of imaginative constipation affects all three works, which again raises the question of why their author finds it so hard to write about September 11. For Amis, we have seen, Islamism is little more than a geo-political black hole but, as the author himself recognizes, this essential lack also makes it impervious to the writer of fiction:

> Islam, as I said, is a total system, and like all such systems it is eerily amenable to satire. But with Islamism, with total malignancy, with total terror and total boredom, irony, even militant irony (which is what satire is), merely shrivels and dies. (p. 87)

If Islamism is reduced to nothing but a 'varnish upon a vacuum' – an illusion superimposed on an illusion (p. 91) – then the risk is that Amis's fiction becomes little more than a varnish on that varnish. On the one hand, then, Islamism is ultimately too small, too superficial a subject for Amis: he leaves himself with nothing to imagine, nothing to satirize or ironize and his work consequently 'shrivels and dies'. On the other, though, it is also too large, too vacuously monolithic to be meaningful: Amis revealingly claims that the main reason why he abandoned 'The Unknown Known' was a suspicion that 'there exists on our planet a kind of human being *who will become* a Muslim in order to pursue suicide mass-murder [our stress – AB and AT]'(p. 87). Finally, then, Islamism becomes little more than an empty placeholder – a 'Known Unknown' to quote the much-maligned epistemologist Donald Rumsfeld – that marks the spot where the real cause or explanation should be. Perhaps this is why 'The Last Days of Mohammed Atta' – a story about exactly the kind of human being who becomes a Muslim in order to pursue suicide mass-murder – turns into an exercise in pure negation: Atta is provided with no political or theological rationale for the September 11 attacks – he is an apostate, a non-believer, and has no interest in a Palestinian state (pp. 101–2) – beyond what he calls the 'core reason' of 'all the killing, all the putting to death' (p. 122). The only really original or un-clichéd thing about the whole story is its conclusion: Atta – for whom 'the thing which is called "World"' is an 'illusion', an 'unreal mockery' (p. 102) – is damned to relive his last day on earth in perpetuity. This small victory in Amis's ongoing war against cliché ultimately turns out to be a somewhat Pyrrhic one, however: what began as an indictment of the toxic malignancy of religious belief ends up imagining a strangely theological, indeed almost Buddhist, afterlife of eternal recurrence for a character, who, it turns out, was an atheist all along. Such are the theological acrobatics this 'not quite' New Atheist novelist is obliged to perform: it may well be that there is no heaven, no paradise, no 72 black-eyed virgins awaiting the martyr – but there is a hell.

## CHAPTER THREE

# PHILIP PULLMAN'S REPUBLIC OF HEAVEN

*Which is it? Is man only God's mistake or God only man's mistake?*[1]

Philip Pullman's *His Dark Materials* trilogy (1995–2000) might be read as an epic, 1,300-page response to Friedrich Nietzsche's provocative question about God and Man. It is well known that Pullman's sequence of novels – ostensibly written for a teenage audience but now widely admired and debated by older readers and critics, both sympathetic and hostile – forcefully confronts the very ground of religious belief. According to Andrew Marr, writing after Pullman was awarded the Whitbread Prize in 2002, *His Dark Materials* can only be read as children's fiction 'in roughly the same way that *A Christmas Carol* is only a fireside fable'.[2] While the trilogy was completed before 9/11, its political anxieties about religious authoritarianism – and particularly the threat to democracy posed by theocracies – anticipate much of the debate regarding the public role of belief that has fomented ever since the attack on the Twin Towers and the subsequent 'War on Terror'. For Pullman himself, it is clear that *His Dark Materials'* hybrid of richly allusive storytelling, post-Darwinian science and Miltonic cosmology constitutes a vast imaginary space in which he can explore the clash between religious faith and scientific rationalism; the dialectics of human freedom and divine rule or free will and determinism; and, ultimately, the very Nietzschean question of whether human beings will ever leave behind their faith in an invisible, ethereal but all-powerful creator. If Pullman is both imaginatively and intellectually sympathetic to the New Atheism – and particularly to the work of Richard Dawkins – this chapter will argue that at the same time *His Dark Materials* remains part of a recognizably Judaeo-Christian tradition of heresy and theological rewriting that stretches from John Milton's *Paradise Lost*, through the Romantic Satanism of William Blake, even up to the pious fantasies of C. S. Lewis. To what extent, then, can Philip Pullman – let alone the human race as a whole – transcend our common religious inheritance?

## 1

In the opinion of many readers, Pullman's epic is more significant for its powerful argument against transcendent religion rather than for its merits as fiction: 'The Christian religion is a very powerful and convincing mistake, that's all', claims one character in the final pages of the trilogy.[3] The fact that these words are spoken by one of the narrative's most sympathetic figures, Mary Malone, an ex-nun who has swapped faith for physics seems to emphasize Pullman's belief in the need for a secular awakening. If, as Philip Goodchild argues, 'the case . . . against religion, morality and reason in the European tradition has been made pre-eminently by Nietzsche', then Pullman's trilogy – comprising *Northern Lights* (published in the US as *The Golden Compass*, 1995); *The Subtle Knife* (1997) and *The Amber Spyglass* (2000) – could be eagerly appropriated as supporting material for the faithless 'prosecution'.[4] Perhaps we might see *His Dark Materials* as a fictional rewriting of Nietzsche's own genealogies of morality, belief and Christian *ressentiment*.

Yet, such a body of evidence is likely to prove uncomfortably conflicting, paradoxical and ambiguous for anybody determined to use the novels as water-tight atheist tracts. On the one hand, *His Dark Materials* suggests a world view that is as viscerally appalled by religion, particularly in its Judaeo-Christian iterations, as any element of Nietzsche's philosophy. It was created by a man whose open hostility to Christianity prompted one noted conservative commentator to describe Pullman as 'the most dangerous author in Britain' (apparently much to the novelist's delight).[5] Such headline-grabbing opprobrium is, however, balanced by the fact that the books have also been defended by people of faith, including the current Archbishop of Canterbury, Dr Rowan Williams. The spiritual leader of the worldwide Anglican Communion has become an unlikely advocate for the series and its successful dramatization by the National Theatre (2004). In fact, he has gone so far as to praise the kind of theological debate prompted by Pullman's narrative and argued that its critique might be welcomed, rather than resented, by orthodox Christians.[6]

At the same time, the controversy surrounding Pullman's trilogy has already inspired a plethora of books, journal articles and profiles.[7] Its author has, by turns, been denounced and praised by Christian critics, championed as a brave advocate of humanist values and damned as a theologian manqué.[8] The fact that the final volume of the trilogy includes the defeat of Pullman's God-figure (a senescent and decrepit angel known as 'the Authority') and the liberation of humanity after a second 'Fall' may be enough to confirm, superficially at least, that Pullman is an anti-Christian propagandist. In a radical contrast to this perspective, however, Donna Freitas and Jason King identify Pullman as the author of 'a contemporary Christian classic' whose work resonates, in particular, with the traditions of liberation theology (*Killing the Impostor God*, p. xxii).

In one sense, though, it does not matter whether Pullman is read as a radical atheist or crypto-Christian because – either way – the novels have a profound debt to the biblical tradition against which they kick so fiercely. Pullman has, of course, publicly identified himself with one strand of New Atheist thought in an essay written in honour of Richard Dawkins.[9] He has also been mischievously frank about the ostensible atheist project of his fiction ('I'm trying to undermine the basis of Christian belief'), but the tale is sometimes at odds with the teller.[10] Not only is his narrative drawn to the scriptures of the so-called Old and New Testaments for aesthetic purposes but, in a number of ways, it is also shaped by Christian notions of the battle between good and evil. Even the now infamous 'murder-of-God' plotline is more richly ambiguous than might superficially appear to be the case. Conservative Christians should be less quick to denounce Pullman for his godlessness and radical atheists less enthusiastic in their celebration of *His Dark Materials* as a clear-cut irreligious epic for our times. For us, Pullman is – of all the New Atheist novelists under review in this book – the one most explicitly dedicated to critiquing the Christian meta-narrative from within. While Martin Amis and Ian McEwan draw attention to what they see as the obvious absurdities of religious practice in a scientific era, Pullman's fiction is caught up with the specific power of religious story-telling. Instead of denying the influence of Jewish and Christian narrative, the novels offer a counter-myth that is at once shamelessly, defiantly heretical and utterly dependent on the story that it repudiates. Despite – or perhaps because of – his loud protestations, Pullman's fictions of atheism resemble nothing so much as a *fictional atheism*, one manufactured to resist conceptions of God rather than the direct claims of a truly transcendent divinity.[11] Perhaps Hugh Rayment-Pickard puts it most succinctly when he says that 'everything in Pullman's counter-Christian myth has been framed by the Christian paradigm. His constellation of concepts and characters only really makes sense when referenced to Christian concepts' (*The Devil's Account*, p. 88).

## 2

*His Dark Materials* is crammed with competing literary allusions: it re-imagines biblical stories, blissfully explores the Western canon for its juiciest motifs and also makes reference to a dazzling plethora of pop cultural sources. Metaphysical poetry, Victorian Sensation fiction, detective stories, popular science, *The Wizard of Oz*, George Lucas's *Star Wars* (1977–83) movies and even the Christian allegory of Lewis's *The Chronicles of Narnia* (1950–6) might all be readily identified as intertexts. Like Britain's most famous twentieth-century writers of theologically informed fantasy fiction, J. R. R. Tolkein and Lewis (for whose work the novelist has expressed a particular aversion), Pullman has created the kind of vivid parallel universe that inspires near-obsessive dedication and apparently limitless interpretation.[12] The stories of Lyra Belacqua (later renamed Lyra Silvertongue) and Will Parry – Pullman's young protagonists – are generically poised between the overlapping worlds of fantasy fiction and the magic realism of novelists such as Jeanette Winterson and Angela Carter. And, like the fiction of Winterson and Carter, Pullman's novels never use the delights of the fantastical as pure escapism from complex ethical problems. The narrative arcs around which *His Dark Materials* is structured draw from the great traditions of myth, romance and realism.

First, and most obviously, the structure of the trilogy echoes that of Lewis's septet. In the first novel, an ostensibly orphaned (and largely unsupervised) child (much like Lucy Pevensie in *The Lion, the Witch and the Wardrobe*) finds her way into a world of adventure and, finally, into a parallel universe. By the time of the final instalment, cosmic forces of good and evil meet for a final, decisive battle that will determine the shape of the universe – a world of liberty or one of eternal suppression. The fact that Pullman and Lewis have strikingly different perspectives on the defining question of God does little to undermine the substantial continuities between their fictional worlds. Lyra and Will begin their own journeys in parallel versions of Oxford: Lyra's home is a kind of Steam-Punk neo-Victorian city, in which she moves freely between the privileged world of Jordan College (the most prestigious seat of learning in her world) and an unruly throng of childish gangs. She is born into a time line in which the Reformation never took place and where the Church (once led by Pope John Calvin in Geneva, a not particularly subtle conceit that allows Pullman to expand his critique of Christianity to include Protestant and Roman Catholic traditions) remains exceptionally powerful without the softening impact of secularization. When Lyra begins a quest to rescue Roger, her abducted best friend, the universe expands as she encounters benign witches, armoured bears (happily blessed with the twin gifts of speech and engineering skills), magical objects (including a compass-like truth-telling device and a knife that slices windows between worlds), soul-eating spectres and assassin priests. She also discovers that her uncle and guardian, Lord Asriel, a mysterious explorer and 'experimental theologian' (the equivalent of a research scientist) is, in fact, her father and that the equally enigmatic and glamorous Mrs Coulter – an agent of the church responsible for the abduction of England's missing children – is her mother. Intriguingly, there are also a number of similarities between Pullman's Lyra and Ian McEwan's Briony Tallis, the central protagonist of *Atonement* (2002): Lyra is a brilliant, inventive liar who discovers the necessity of truth-telling; Briony believes that she is committed to telling the truth but comes to terms with her own untruths. Both characters, likewise, are motivated by the desire to atone for perceived failings and, in particular, their tacit roles in the death of a friend: Briony's lie not only separates Robbie and Cecilia but condemns the former to prison and, perhaps, to his death as a soldier at Dunkirk; Lyra accidentally leads her friend Roger to Lord Asriel who sacrifices him for the sake of his desire to move across worlds.

Will, introduced into the narrative in *The Subtle Knife*, volume 2 of the trilogy, is from (as Pullman quaintly puts it) 'the universe we know'. After all, Will's narrative begins in circumstances that echo the traditions of social realism rather than fantasy fiction: he is a troubled teenager, terrified that social services will separate him from his mother, who appears to be suffering from an acute mental illness.

Will fights (and accidentally kills) an intruder who is pursuing his missing father. Running away from the suburbs of Winchester, he arrives in Oxford and stumbles through a window that leads to yet another parallel world, where he encounters Lyra. The strikingly quotidian atmosphere of Will's world (and ours) is heightened by the fact that Lyra is from a universe in which each person's soul is visible in the form of an animal, a constant companion and confidante for every human being. These *daemons* continually shape-shift until adolescence when they settle on a form that best reflects the character of their human companion: a bird, for example, signifies spiritual freedom; dogs tend to indicate subservient tendencies. In keeping with the great traditions of the folk tale, Lyra and Will uncover secrets about their own identities and become enmeshed in a war between forces of freedom and oppression: the end of the trilogy recasts them as a kind of modern Adam and Eve, faced with temptation and given ultimate responsibility for the well-being of all creation.

Who, besides Lewis, are the chief literary precursors for Pullman's trilogy? The novel, more than any other narrative genre, has been identified as particularly democratic in its ability to assimilate plural sources, voices and references.[13] For the New Atheist novelists, as we have seen, such belief in fiction's liberating power to say anything and everything is elevated to the status of an article of faith. Pullman's work consciously celebrates its status as one text among many and is open about the fact that its own story finds meaning in its borrowings from a vast array of other narratives. After all, with the exception of its epilogue, every chapter in *The Amber Spyglass* is tagged with a literary epigram: Pullman quotes figures as diverse as the author of Job, Pindar, Edmund Spenser, Andrew Marvell, George Herbert, John Milton, Samuel Taylor Coleridge, Emily Dickinson and John Ruskin. This hefty body of citations sit in the narrative like an arsenal stockpiled for the trilogy's final confrontation with its own *Ur*-text, the Bible. Pullman's narrative, though peppered with biblical references, overtly writes *against* conventionally religious interpretations of the authorized body of Jewish-Christian literature; but it also acknowledges a profound imaginative debt to these scriptures – a debt that would also have been owned by almost all of the writers that he so liberally quotes.

*His Dark Materials* has, however, a brace of particular literary inspirations that take precedence over and above this vast library of rival references. The first, and most explicit, of these twin influences is John Milton's *Paradise Lost* (1667). Milton's epic of 'man's first disobedience' itself wrestles with and rewrites the account of human- ity's fall from grace in Genesis.[14] This act of interpretation might, in itself, be read as audacious in that it departs from the original text despite its avowed intention to 'assert eternal providence, / And justify the ways of God to men' (Book 1, ll. 25–6). Pullman's narra- tive, ostensibly at least, seems to invert this objective in its open hostility to any force – human or divine – that aspires to omnipo- tence. The poem dramatizes the clash between the armies of the rebel angel Satan with those of God the Father and concludes with Adam and Eve's exile from Eden after they succumb to temptation. Pullman takes this mythic framework and recasts it with a series of figures who resemble Milton's *dramatis personae*. For example, Lord Asriel, a renegade scholar determined to pursue truth (and, less honourably, power) at any expense, is the closest figure in Pullman's narrative to Milton's 'apostate angel' (Book 1, l. 125), though not the only char- acter who is touched by the desire for freedom. In the final volume, Will and Lyra take on the identities of the world's first couple, Adam and Eve, when they face a double-veiled temptation. Other figures echo Milton's cast of angels and devils, but it is not solely at the level of character that *His Dark Materials* reworks its parent text. Pullman's life-long love of the poem coupled with a sceptical sensi- bility prompted him to ground his narrative of liberating rebellion in Milton's epic. This intertextual relation is announced in the epigram to the first book in the trilogy, *Northern Lights*, an extended quota- tion from Book II of *Paradise Lost*:

> Into this wild abyss,
> The womb of nature and perhaps her grave,
> Of neither sea, nor shore, nor air, nor fire,
> But all these in their pregnant causes mixed
> Confus'dly, and which thus must ever fight,
> Unless the almighty maker them ordain
> His dark materials to create more worlds,
> Into this wild abyss the wary fiend
> Stood on the brink of hell and looked awhile,
> Pondering his voyage . . . (Book II, ll. 910–19)

In these lines, Satan, defeated and exiled, broods on the vast chasm that separates his new province from heaven, and considers the possibility that out of the chaos might emerge a new world or worlds. 'His dark materials' are the substance out of which God creates the new world of earth, to be populated by humanity, a rival and possible ally, in Satan's eyes, to the rebel angels. Pullman reinterprets these 'dark materials' in multiple ways: they might be 'dark matter', the very stuff of the universe that fascinates contemporary physicists or – in the novels' defining metaphor – the mysterious substance known as 'Dust' that seems to generate consciousness and creativity in all sentient beings.

In a recent essay on Milton's Biblicism, Michael Lieb reminds us that *Paradise Lost* has a debt to Revelation (Chapter 12. 7–9, in particular) as well as to its more obvious grounding in Genesis 1–3.[15] Similarly, *His Dark Materials* is informed by both the first and last books of the Bible. It, like *Paradise Lost*, is also an apocalyptic text in a double sense: the narrative both explores apocalypse in its primary meaning as revelation (moments of epiphany occur through-out a trilogy that is fascinated by the possibility of bringing to light that which is hidden) and in its secondary (though, perhaps, more widely recognized) signification as that which attends to last things, the end of the world, the representation of death, judgement, heaven and hell. The idea of a war in heaven – on which subsequent stories of the fall of Satan are based – and of a final conflict between good and evil as narrated in Revelation is conflated and replayed explicitly in *The Amber Spyglass*. King Ogunwe, a minor character who rallies to the cause of Lord Asriel and his eclectic, ragtag army that chal-lenges the 'Authority', explains the coming war to Lyra as a just rebellion against a fraudulent ruler (*The Amber Spyglass*, p. 222). This trope of uprising against a usurping divinity in an apocalyptic battle also demonstrates Pullman's affinity with the writing of William Blake.[16] Indeed, *His Dark Materials'* second defining parent text is Blake's heretical rereading of Milton's classic poem in *The Marriage of Heaven and Hell* (1790–3). The Romantic poet famously – and, for many critics, somewhat scandalously – cast his predecessor not as unequivocally devout but as 'a true Poet and of the Devil's party without knowing it'.[17] This bold, counter-intuitive understand-ing has shaped the reception of Milton for the last two centuries but few interpreters have been as deeply engaged with Blake's ideas as Pullman.

By identifying so explicitly with Blake's subversive take on the poem, *His Dark Materials* can be associated with what Valentine

Cunningham has named the great tradition of English literary heresy.[18] Although heresy is frequently regarded as the expression of irreligious ideas, it almost always originates in the desire of the heretic to *purify* religious practice – to return it to a state of integrity – rather than to abandon the faith altogether.[19] Peter Berger has argued that the shift in attitudes towards dissenting thought is one of the major cultural changes that signify the birth of modernity. *'For premodern man, heresy is a possibility – usually a rather remote one; for modern man, heresy typically becomes a necessity'*, claims Berger.[20] Pullman, whose work is a product of the *post*modern era, is writing in a context of supposedly advanced secularization in which the authority of religious institutions has waned to such an extent that it cannot be assumed that the majority of his readers will even recognize biblical allusions. There is a marked and defamiliarizing difference between the epoch of religious tyranny into which Lyra is born – a parallel world in which the Church or 'Magisterium' controls every aspect of cultural life, including education, government and scientific endeavour – and the (ostensibly at least) liberal, tolerant Britain of the 1990s in which Pullman wrote the trilogy. In his study of the loss of religious faith over the last 200 years, Callum Brown, for example, argues that secularization in early twenty-first-century Britain is 'not merely the continuing decline of organised Christianity, but the death of the culture which formerly conferred Christian identity upon the British people as a whole'.[21]

Perhaps literature – and particularly the novel – has become the primary space in which once deep-rooted, if widely forgotten and deracinated, religious ideas can be revisited, tested and reshaped. Cunningham goes on to argue that 'literature in English thrives on heresy' and what he names as the 'grand creative principle' of heterodox thought certainly animates *His Dark Materials* ('Introduction: The Necessity of Heresy', p. 1, p. 12). This playfully dissenting approach to revered texts is most explicit in Pullman's Blakean interpretation of the figure of Satan. Blake believed that Milton had an unconscious allegiance to Satan and his rebel angels that was not indicative of immorality but a sign of authentic spirituality. Of Blake's critical interpretation of the poem, Lucy Newlyn notes that the wayward writer 'not only splits the psyche in two, producing a struggle for power between the tyrannical conscious and the oppressed unconscious; he also splits *Paradise Lost* in two, producing a subtext and a supertext'. This split, suggests Newlyn, is key to the poem's reception history 'because it makes the conflict between different kinds of reading central to the act of interpretation' (*Paradise Lost and the Romantic Reader*, pp. 39–40). In rewriting *Paradise Lost* in novel form, Pullman plays a part in this evolving reception history – a story of interpretation that became particularly dynamic in the twentieth century, re-energized by very different responses to the Romantics.

Pullman was preceded by his great imaginative adversary, C. S. Lewis, not just as a writer of religiously inflected fantasy fiction but also as a reader of Milton's poem. Lewis argues in his *A Preface to Paradise Lost* (1942) that our understanding of the poem was distorted by Blake and his contemporaries: 'rebellion and pride,' notes Lewis, 'came, in the romantic age, to be admired for their own sake'. For Lewis – writing openly as a Christian reader – Milton's status had been diminished by the defiant heterodoxy of Blake and his inheritors.[22] In response to one critic's suggestion that readers must 'disentangle' Milton's 'lasting originality' from the alleged 'theological rubbish' of his work, Lewis makes the stark claim that 'Milton's thought, when purged of its theology, does not exist' (p. 65). The idea that any reading of the poem can simply transcend its Christian implications (including one presumes a reshaping of the narrative as a wholly secular novel) is, according to this view, an impossibility.[23] Perhaps, by the same token, *His Dark Materials* – as a heterodox reading of *Paradise Lost* – cannot escape its own historico-theological origins. Could Pullman's trilogy exist without the very 'theological rubbish' it, too, seeks to throw out?

In many ways, Pullman's hostility to conventional religion as a basis for reading the poem is not without modern precedent either. If Lewis is Milton's most eminent modern Christian apologist, then William Empson – one of the truly distinctive voices in English literary criticism – is arguably the best-known twentieth-century religious sceptic (before Pullman) to engage with *Paradise Lost*. In *Milton's God* (1961), Empson admits to a surprise at the 'revival of Christianity among literary critics' that prefigures a similar sense of alarm experienced by some sceptical thinkers in the early twenty-first century. His reading of Milton is informed, he notes from the beginning of the study, by a profound moral antipathy for Christian belief: 'I think the traditional God of Christianity very wicked, and have done since I was at school', states Empson.[24] Indeed, in the concluding chapter, a critique of Christian theology, he advances the view that Milton's God, however flawed, is morally 'very much better than the traditional God of Christianity, not worse as has so often been said in recent times'. 'The Christian God the Father', claims Empson, 'the God of Tertullian, Augustine and Aquinas, is the wickedest thing yet invented by the black heart of man' (*Milton's God*, p. 272, p. 250).[25] What, if anything, then, does *His Dark Materials* add to the heretical tradition from which it emerges?

## 3

For us, Pullman clearly continues the doubting trajectory of Blake and Empson in his own heretical epic. His own brand of faithful scepticism thus echoes the neo-Romantic sympathies of other novelists associated with New Atheism, including a near mystical enthusiasm for nature and, more pertinently, a rebellious contempt for self-ordained authority. One of the key differences between Lewis and Pullman, for instance, is their interpretation of Satan. If Lewis sees Milton's Satan as a proud and ultimately somewhat pathetic figure whom it is deeply misguided to respect (*Preface*, p. 102), Pullman's narrative, by contrast, displays a Blakean sympathy for the devil and his bid for freedom. Pullman begins his introduction to Oxford University Press' illustrated edition of *Paradise Lost* (2005) with the unverifiable folk tale of an ageing eighteenth-century squire listening to a reading of Milton's poem. The squire's enthusiasm for Lucifer and hope that this 'damned fine fellow might win', is a response heartily endorsed by the novelist (*Paradise Lost*, p. 1).

At the same time, Pullman's alternative reading of the poem magnifies the ambiguities of its potentially unorthodox elements. Whereas Lewis emphasizes Milton's theology of grace and the goodness of God, *His Dark Materials* is concerned with humanity in terms of its fragile, finite, flesh-bound beauty. Pullman and Lewis's rival interpretations of Christian texts, including the scriptures and *Paradise Lost*, might be read as an index of secularization during the half-century since the publication of *The Chronicles of Narnia*. In an article comparing the two writers, for example, Naomi Wood shows how Pullman's attitude towards obedience stands in stark contrast to that of Lewis, whose understanding of sin and obedience is mediated by a conservative reading of the book of Genesis and *Paradise Lost*: Pullman, she argues, 'retells the Genesis story as a prohibition against becoming autonomous, free, adult'.[26]

Milton, Lewis and Pullman's shared fascination with the human propensity for transgression echoes ancient and unresolved theological debates. Alan Jacobs notes, in his commendable cultural history of the doctrine, that 'original sin' generates more 'hostility' than any other piece of religious teaching.[27] The idea, in its multiple Christian forms, emphasizes that human beings are born into a world of sin because of the actions of their first ancestors, Adam and Eve, and reasons that individuals cannot transcend this taint by their own efforts. Such a doctrine of inherited guilt is not universally accepted by Christians and, not surprisingly, Pullman represents it as particularly pernicious. Yet, the story of humanity's fall from grace continues to beguile, even as it infuriates, this sceptical writer. Indeed, the idea of the fall becomes both a vital structural motif in Pullman's critique of traditional theism and a clue to his continuing reliance on Jewish and Christian narrative. For Pullman, the substance known as 'Dust' – invisible to the human eye but fundamental to all conscious life – is a complex motif of sin, human intelligence and the very stuff of the universe.

For Pullman, as he stresses in his public debate with Rowan Williams, what is interesting about the Fall is the relationship between consciousness, self-knowledge and spirituality it emblematizes.[28] According to Williams, it is a religious fallacy to suppose that believers can somehow make the reverse journey of Adam and Eve and return to the Garden of Eden (*Darkness Illuminated*, p. 91). This understanding of the Fall explicitly denies the possibility of recreating a pre-lapsarian state but opens up, instead, the hope of grace. However, *His Dark Materials* is explicitly hostile to the notion of unwarranted, unearned grace. Every part of Pullman's multiverse seems to have experienced a fall: even the world of the peaceful *mulefa*, befriended by Mary Malone, in which the natural order appears harmonious, is damaged: Mary becomes aware that 'some virtue had gone out of the world . . . the wheel-pod trees were dying' (*The Amber Spyglass*, p. 139). While this element of story focuses on environmental degradation rather than theological connivance, Pullman's language is, not coincidentally, post-lapsarian. In fact, there is a real tension in Pullman's trilogy between the necessity of knowledge – of embracing what might be called 'sin' – and the fact that any world in which a fall has taken place is also subject to injustice. Where does this tension come from?

'Milton's version of the Fall story', argues C. S. Lewis, 'is substantially that of St Augustine, which is that of the Church as a whole'

(*Preface*, p. 66). This affirmation of Milton's theological orthodoxy is likely to surprise many, if not most, readers whose encounter with *Paradise Lost* is shaped by Blake's reading of the poem as instinctively transgressive. Lewis, following Augustine, notes that the 'perversion' of 'good things' occurs 'when a conscious creature becomes more interested in itself than in God . . . and wishes to exist "on its own" . . . This is the sin of Pride' (p. 66). Such creaturely self-consciousness is vital to the (a-)theology of *His Dark Materials* and is addressed directly in *Northern Lights*. In the climax of this opening volume, Lyra is reunited with her father, Lord Asriel, who, in an echo of Satan's incarceration in Book I of *Paradise Lost*, is temporarily imprisoned because of his challenge to the religious authorities. Asriel responds to Lyra's questions about the mysterious substance known as 'Dust' – which is invisible to the human eye and constellates around human beings from adolescence onwards – by reading her the story of the Fall, as recounted in Genesis. Pullman deftly pastiches the style of the Authorised (King James) Version in a story that nevertheless represents a significant departure from the canonical narrative. As in 'our' version of Genesis 3, Eve is tempted by a serpent. However, in this iteration of the story, the tempter connects the discovery of good and evil with a liberating knowledge of the soul:

> For God doth know that in the day ye eat thereof, then your eyes shall be opened, and your daemons shall assume their true forms, and ye shall be as gods, knowing good and evil . . . But when the man and the woman knew their own daemons, they knew a great change had come upon them, for until that moment it had seemed that they were at one with all the creatures of the earth and the air, and there was no difference between them:

> 'And they saw the difference, and they knew good and evil; and they were ashamed, and they sewed fig leaves together to cover their nakedness'.[29]

Whereas the biblical narrative of our own version of Genesis 3 tropes the Fall in terms of sin, exile and incompletion, Pullman constructs it in neo-Romantic terms as a crucial image of human self-definition and personal liberty. Naomi Wood argues that this vision of the fall insists that 'God's prohibition demeans both God and man: warning Adam and Eve away from the Tree of Knowledge, God seems only to want them ignorant to protect his own status' ('Paradise Lost and Found', p. 248). Pullman's rewriting of the Fall narrative certainly emphasizes the coincidence of shame, prohibition and unfettered self-knowledge with a direct challenge to divine authority. In his version, the story offers a mythic explanation for the final shape of a person's *daemon* (the visible, animal form of the soul) and underlines the idea that humanity needs to fall in order to arrive at maturity.

Perhaps Pullman's narrative is an example of what Lewis means when he argues that *Paradise Lost* 'gives the great central tradition' of Christianity by inviting its readers 'to join in this great ritual *mimesis* of the Fall' (*A Preface to* Paradise Lost, p. 92). Pullman subverts this 'ritual' imitation, however, by re-presenting it as a form of Gnostic interpretation of humanity's challenge to the divine. Although the term Gnosticism describes a wide and diverging mode of religious thought, one key strand emphasizes the idea that an evil, oppressive god holds humanity in chains until challenged. Adam and Eve, in this Gnostic model, lose favour with their God (who is closer, in some traditions, to the figure of Satan) but they gain immense esoteric, spiritual knowledge. In his public debate with Rowan Williams, Pullman, citing the pop culture examples of *The X-Files* and *The Matrix* revealingly invokes '[t]he great salience of gnostic feelings, gnostic sentiments and ways of thinking in our present world' (*Darkness Illuminated*, p. 88). Can *His Dark Materials* be more profitably read as a work of postmodern Gnosticism rather than as an atheist text?

The Gnostic implications of a 'happy' fall as a powerful alternative to Christian nostalgia for lost innocence are emblematized throughout the trilogy. Lyra's shocking discovery, in the frozen wilderness of Bolvangar, of the true purpose of the mass kidnappings accentuates this idea. These lost children are subject to a violent process known as 'intercision' which separates a child from its *daemon* (*Northern Lights*, p. 274). This horrific experimental practice is intended to prevent sin entering the lives of adolescents or, in the seductive Mrs Coulter's terms, 'daemons bring all sort of troublesome thoughts and feelings, and that's what lets Dust in' (*Northern Lights*, p. 285). It is significant here that *intercision* – the severing of a child from its daemon – is a near homonym of *intercession*, the act of prayer for others. Although the sequence at Bolvangar draws its imagery from amoral or cruel scientific experiments – and most specifically the work of Nazi scientists – it might also be read as a metaphor of religious rites of passage.[30] In Wood's view, a recurrent premise of

Pullman's fiction is that an 'overvaluation of innocence' inherited from the Victorians 'actually limits and even harms those whose innocence is ostensibly being protected' ('Dismembered Starlings and Neutered Minds', p. 17). The idea that innocence has become a fetish of bourgeois society – rather than a state of grace – is powerfully adumbrated across the trilogy.

The trilogy finds its resolution in a recapitulation of the Adam and Eve story: indeed, Lyra's own significance as a kind of second *first* woman, a new Eve, is prophesied in the first two volumes of the story and fulfilled in *The Amber Spyglass*. In *The Subtle Knife*, one of the witches who protects Lyra proclaims that the child "'will be the mother – she will be life – mother – she will disobey" and, more explicitly, that she will become "Eve, again! Mother Eve!"'.[31] After the defeat of the Authority and his armies, Lyra and Will escape to the idyllic (but fallen) world of the Mulefa, where they are reunited with Mary Malone. In this lapsed nun and physicist, Pullman has conflated a number of biblical figures: her name encodes both Mary mother of Christ and Mary Magdalene, the penitent sinner; she is also the tempter. The ex-nun becomes a benign version of the serpent in the Genesis narrative: her own story of unconversion from Christianity, itself rooted in her desire to experience erotic love and sensuality, prompts the two friends to recognize their love for one another. In pursuit of their daemons, from whom they have been separated, Will and Lyra express their love in some form of physical contact that is elided from the narrative itself. Lyra and Will have 'come into their inheritance' as 'the true image of what human beings always could be' but this is not represented as a cause for regret or nostalgia (*The Amber Spyglass*, p. 497). Instead their ambiguous act of love is figured as salvific and Pullman uses a language of epiphany that conflates spiritual and scientific vocabulary to represent a world transformed by human agency. Mary looks out at the stars with her improvised telescope (the titular amber spyglass) and witnesses creation renewed: 'The Dust pouring down from the stars had found a living home again, and these children-no-longer-children, saturated with love, were the cause of it all' (*The Amber Spyglass*, p. 497). Pullman's account of the Fall – as a recurrent, rather than singular historical phenomenon – is positive, even celebratory. In *The Amber Spyglass*, original sin is transfigured into original blessing – though Pullman's narrative does not escape questions of sacrifice, exile and the desire for transcendence.

PHILIP PULLMAN'S REPUBLIC OF HEAVEN

## 4

What prompted the contrarian right-wing columnist (and brother of New Atheist Christopher) Peter Hitchens, in a *Mail on Sunday* article published in 2002, to describe Pullman as 'the most dangerous author in Britain'? Why do some conservative Christians regard *His Dark Materials* as a particularly potent threat to their faith? The novelist is clearly a spirited critic of religion and what he perceives as its associated evils (an unholy trinity of immaturity, irresponsibility and injustice). But it is unlikely that his fiction – whatever its heterodox understanding of original sin – would have been so controversial on this basis alone. Literary representations of institutional belief as antiquated, authoritarian and arrogant are, after all, far from new. Holy hypocrites and cruel clergymen have populated English prose fiction since its birth in the eighteenth century; and, during the heyday of the novel, Victorian writers such as Charles Dickens and Charlotte Brontë, now regarded as cosily canonical, were criticized in religious periodicals for their apparent irreverence and disrespect. Perhaps Pullman might have received either a simple chiding or warm critical handshake for his novels' mischievous, morally outraged anti-clericalism had this Miltonic sequence concluded with the first two volumes. *The Amber Spyglass*, however, considerably ups the New Atheist ante by choosing to focus on the murder of God or, to be more precise, the death of a self-appointed deity. The fact that this deicide – in a work of fiction ostensibly aimed at teenage readers – is characterized as necessary and heroic is likely to have stunned, initially at least, even those liberal believers who shared the writer's antipathy for despotic religious leaders and blind faith to a near totalitarian cause.

*Northern Lights* and *The Subtle Knife* have little to say about God; indeed, the specific theological beliefs practised by the powerful, and near omnipresent clergy, in Lyra's universe (with the exception of the General Oblation Board's strategic obsession with sin and the onset of adolescence) remain tantalizingly vague. It is clear in these first two novels that the Magisterium is corrupt, bullying and powerful but this is balanced by the fact that the whole of the mainstream adult world is represented as inadequate, morally compromised and guided more by fear than love or happiness. Lyra's parents are glamorous and dynamic but utterly selfish; Will's father is absent and his mother psychologically damaged; generations of irresponsible

71

alchemists in the parallel, Italianate world of Cittàzze have brought about suffering for their children. The only adults to be figured as decent, caring and truly free are those who exist on the fringes of society: in Lyra's Oxford, the canal-dwelling, travelling Gyptian people are associated with liberty, generosity and honesty; Lee Scorseby, the Texan balloonist gun-for-hire (surely a spiritual cousin to George Lucas's Han Solo), is both outlaw and unlikely saviour. In Will's world – most closely allied to our own – the former nun and renegade physicist Mary Malone, marginalized by her peers, is the only adult who appears to be trustworthy. *The Amber Spyglass*, however, turns its gaze away from the failings of Lyra and Will's earthly parent-figures and towards the ultimate supposed parent: God himself.

Georg Lukács's influential classification of the novel form as 'the epic of a world abandoned by God' (*Theory of the Novel*, p. 88) is violently transformed in the trilogy's final volume: Pullman's worlds have emphatically not been abandoned by the deity, but are rather overseen by a tyrannical 'god'-figure. This tyrant is eventually destroyed by brave rebels, who are not simply hedonistic immoralists but seekers after justice and truth. In Pullman's model, 'god' is an impostor who clings to power, and his so-called subjects would be free if only he chose to abandon them.

The role of the godhead is doubled in *The Amber Spyglass*. The declining influence of 'god' in Pullman's world is contrasted by the figure of his Regent, the angel Metatron, the Authority's inheritor. In a speech by Lord Asriel, Pullman makes it explicit that he is drawing on the figure of Enoch from Jewish mystical (and mythical) tradition (*The Amber Spyglass*, p. 393). Indeed, Pullman makes a number of playful references to religious-mystic tradition in his angelic figures: the rebel angel Baruch, for example, has a name that bears a double allusion to the Hebrew word for 'blessed' and to the first name of Spinoza, the great humanist philosopher. Metatron seems to fascinate pop cultural figures engaged in religious satire: he also appears, for example, in Kevin Smith's *Dogma* (1999), played by Alan Rickman as the laconic (and benign) voice of God. In Pullman's narrative, however, he symbolizes the dangerous possibility of a return to religious fundamentalism: 'god' might be weakened or dying, but new forms of authority are ready to take his place (*The Amber Spyglass*, p. 393).

Metatron might be read, then, as a metaphor for the human ambition to rule as gods rather than to live justly in the fellowship of others. As the heir of the Authority, Metatron is the closest that *His Dark Materials* comes to representing the second person of an alternative, *un*-holy trinity. Significantly, he is represented as the anti-thesis of Christ: where the Jesus of the gospels is fully human (however we choose to interpret claims about his divinity), Pullman's Metatron is jealous of those who have a mortal human frame; where Jesus is self-denying and gentle, Metatron is lascivious and brutal. Indeed, his own destruction is precipitated by desire for Marisa Coulter who, together with Lord Asriel, sacrifices herself to defeat the threat of a new epoch of tyranny.

One way in which the narrative traces the corrupting influence of belief in the Authority and his reign is the moral regeneration of Marisa Coulter. She only becomes ethically generous once she loses her allegiance to the Authority. In the first two volumes of the trilogy, Mrs Coulter is characterized as a devoted (if self-interested) agent of the Magisterium, the authoritarian and all-powerful Church of Lyra's world (though it is clear that her loyalty is primarily a means of self-advancement). However, her sudden conversion – an affective change brought about by previously repressed maternal feelings – places her in opposition to the church by the beginning of *The Amber Spyglass*. She is neither an ally of Lord Asriel, her former lover, nor a member of the faithful. The newly renegade Mrs Coulter becomes the mouthpiece for rational – even devout – scepticism:

> Well, where is God [. . .] if he's alive? And why doesn't he speak any more? At the beginning of the world, God walked in the garden and spoke with Adam and Eve. Then he began to withdraw, and Moses only heard his voice. Later, in the time of Daniel, he was aged – he was the Ancient of Days [. . .] Is he still alive, at some inconceivable age, decrepit and demented, unable to think or act or speak and unable to die, a rotten hulk? And if that *is* his condition, wouldn't it be the most merciful thing, the truest proof of our love for God, to seek him out and give him the gift of death? (*The Amber Spyglass*, pp. 344–5)

This passage conflates competing scriptural and modern philosophical concepts of divinity. The description of the Authority as 'the Ancient of Days' is an allusion to the dream-visions of the prophet Daniel. In his dream, the visionary sees a white-haired figure seated on a throne 'flaming with fire' who is attended by 'ten thousand times ten thousand' (Daniel 7. 9–10). The coolly delivered call for the mercy killing of a senescent and impotent God is framed as an act of religious adoration ('the truest proof of our love for God') and echoes the 'death of God' theologies of the 1960s. It also echoes nineteenth-century anxieties – indeed, anger – about the *deus absconditus* and, in particular, the philosophy of Friedrich Nietzsche. In *The Gay Science*, Nietzsche – one of Gadamer's 'masters of suspicion', a modernist holy trinity that also includes Sigmund Freud and Karl Marx – famously depicts a Madman announcing, not simply the death, but the murder of God: 'we have killed him – you and I'.[32]

The words of the Madman read as an uncanny foreshadowing of the literal killing of the deity – or pseudo-deity – at the end of Pullman's trilogy. It is seldom remarked that Nietzsche's depiction of the murder of God is more ambiguous and mournful than might be obvious: the Madman seems both ecstatic and melancholic about the prospect of life without divinity. At the same time, however, he is utterly clear about who is responsible for that divinity's demise. For the Madman, only humanity can kill God – and they must live with the consequence of such an act. To our eyes, Pullman's hostility to religion is an echo of this tradition and, just as Nietzsche's madman announced that God had been murdered, so does his late twentieth-century inheritor come close to literalizing this idea with the defeat of the Authority. The act of divine murder that the two young protagonists are charged with in *The Amber Spyglass* – armed with a knife that is known as *Æsahættr*, a word that one character claims 'sounds as if it means *god-destroyer*' (*The Subtle Knife*, p. 286) – proves unnecessary because the Authority has become so weak that he simply disintegrates, crumbling with a sigh of relief into oblivion. Instead of murder, they simply hasten an inevitable death. Rather than approaching this ageing figure with aggression, the children help a god they neither recognize nor fear. Indeed, the whole passage is figured with pathos as Will and Lyra help 'the ancient of days out of his crystal cell . . . and to their dismay his form began to loosen and dissolve' dying with 'a sigh of the most profound and exhausted relief' (*The Amber Spyglass*, p. 432). The Authority, finally, is merely 'a mystery dissolving in mystery' in an episode that seems to symbolize the weightlessness or vulnerability of God (*The Amber Spyglass*, p. 432). The fact that this being – once god-like if not God – is helped to die by two children who act without malice (indeed, they are presented as guiltless) is symbolically important. Such a symbolic death, richly suggestive of the paper-thin presence of God in the modern mind, implies that no real ontological violence is necessary to rid humanity of an oppressive belief in providence. In the end, this wizened figure has outlived his time and, by implication, so too has the whole concept of a benign authority, a divine father who oversees the lives of mortal beings with mercy and infinite care.

So, is Pullman really killing off God – even in the sense of an intellectual leave-taking of the concept of a supreme being? Is the death of the Authority a fictional equivalent of Sam Harris's claim that 'words like "God" . . . must go the way of "Apollo" and "Baal," or they will unmake the world' (*End of Faith*, p. 14)? Other critics – such as Donna Freitas and Jason King – also emphasize the Nietzschean qualities of *His Dark Materials*. According to Freitas and King, though, Nietzsche is not attacking theism *per se* but a particular kind of image of God (*Killing the Impostor God*, pp. 17–18): they go on to argue that, while Pullman certainly resembles 'a protest atheist', he kills one God only to replace him with another, in the form of the nebulous 'Dust' (pp. 19–20). To be sure, Pullman himself acknowledges a similarity between the death of the 'Authority' in *His Dark Materials* – a fraudulent God – and the claim of Meister Eckhart that in order to find God, one must first be free of 'God' (*Darkness Illuminated*, p. 58). Any outrage we may feel over the death of God may be misplaced, then, since it is made clear that the 'god' of Pullman's multiverse is no such thing. Balthamos, the rebel angel in *The Amber Spyglass*, tells Will of the Authority and his different names: 'The Authority, God, the Creator, the Lord, Yahweh, El Adonai, the King, the Father, the Almighty – those were all names he gave himself' (*The Amber Spyglass*, p. 33). This feared figure is not the prime mover in all history, though, nor is he authentically omniscient. In Balthamos's words, 'He was never the creator. He was an angel like ourselves [. . .] He told those who came after him that he had created them, but it was a lie' (*The Amber Spyglass*, pp. 33–4).

The Authority actually resembles the 'ancient of days' far less than he does Milton's 'apostate angel'. His claim to be self-authored, preceding not only other angels but Dust – or matter – itself echoes Lewis's interpretation of Satan's arrogance in *Paradise Lost*. The 'root of his whole predicament', argues Lewis, is 'the doctrine that he is a self-existent being, not a derived being, a creature' (*A Preface to*

Paradise Lost, p. 97). This is also true of the Authority who denies his own creaturely identity in order to rise above creation. If it is more obvious to cast Asriel as Pullman's Satan – his defiance, charisma and ruthlessness all resonate with Romantic iterations of the Satanic rebel – it might, in fact, be more credible to read the 'Authority' as occupying this role. The picture that Balthamos paints of his tyrannical ancestor is both less and more Miltonic than Pullman may have intended. Rather than simply depose a despotic, dictatorial god, the narrative mocks the aspirations of a being who would become God. God and Satan, in this description, are uncannily close. Is the Authority the real villain – or is the truest wrongdoing committed by those desperate to preserve their life solely in order to leach power and authority for their own unholy purpose?

Ultimately, the god defeated by Pullman's heroes has little real resemblance to the God of Jewish or Christian revelation. Terry Eagleton has reminded us that the pre-modern Christian world view held a much stronger view of the *transcendence* of God that did not simply view divinity as another category of being. According to this view, God is far less interested in control than in love.[33] The kind of god imagined in *His Dark Materials* is a figure who has only limited omniscience; he has institutional power but lacks real transcendence. In many ways, he resembles an Enlightenment notion of a divinity who is instrumentalist, impersonal, bound by the limits of human reason and utterly dependent on a mode of authority that proves to be frail. Significantly, a celebration of embodiment and the material world is at the heart of Pullman's critique. Lord Asriel celebrates human beings for their incarnate nature – the Authority's angelic forces, he notes, are disadvantaged because they are not made of flesh and bone and envy those who possess mortal bodies (*The Amber Spyglass*, pp. 394–5). This line ostensibly seems to attack the otherworldliness of Christian belief. Yet, Christianity itself – as opposed to the brand of Gnostic god deposed in *The Amber Spyglass* – is a religious tradition rooted in belief in the incarnation: Christ signifies the mysterious connection between transcendence and immanence rather than the idea, common among certain strands of Gnosticism, that the flesh itself is inherently evil. Whether or not this claim is merely theological wishful thinking, it is clear that *His Dark Materials* cannot be deemed free of Christian traces: its critique of 'Christianity' is paradoxically carried out from a more authentically Christian perspective.

## 5

So, does Pullman really belong to the Satanic school, the Devil's Party? It is striking, for example, that Graham Holderness is able to claim that the novelist – *pace* Milton – is 'of God's party, without knowing it' ('The Undiscovered Country', p. 289). Such an impudently Christian appropriation of *His Dark Materials* is primarily based on an episode in *The Amber Spyglass* in which Lyra and Will willingly enter the land of the dead – the supposed 'heaven' of Pullman's multiverse – in order to rescue Roger, Lyra's murdered best friend. This instalment certainly demonstrates the theological ambiguity of the trilogy. Death itself is represented as democratic ('Everyone comes here, kings, queens, murderers, poets, children') but emphatically does not lead to a place of blessed relief (people who commit suicide in the hope of peace discover that 'nothing had changed except for the worse, and this time there was no escape', *The Amber Spyglass*, pp. 301–2). The world of the dead is no heaven but 'a prison camp' and the protagonists' willing descent into this hellish world echoes both classical accounts of Katabasis (Orpheus and Eurydice, for example) and, more pertinently, the Christian tradition of Jesus Christ's harrowing of hell (*The Amber Spyglass*, p. 35). In choosing to enter the land of the dead, Lyra has to be separated from her daemon, the embodiment of her soul. This moment fuses Classical and Christian motifs. She will be taken across a river by a deathly boatman – an allusion to Styx – and struggles like Christ in the garden of Gethsemane with the suffering that she must face. The land of the dead is overseen by Harpies: the terrifying hybrid bird-women figures of Greek mythology. Just as Christ faced a tortuous estrangement from God the Father, Lyra must accept a painful separation from her *daemon*, Pantalaimon. Similarly, Lyra's desire to free 'all' these poor dead ghost-kids' from the colourless, disembodied gloom of their drab eternity is Christ-like (*The Amber Spyglass*, p. 319; see also Holderness's 'The Undiscovered Country', pp. 276–92). The biblical echoes are intensified in the epigraph to Chapter 23 ('No Way Out'), which is taken from the Gospel of John (8. 32): 'And ye shall know the truth, and the truth shall make you free' (*The Amber Spyglass*, p. 321).

Pullman's synthesis of Christian and Classical sources underlines the trilogy's concern with heterodox readings of mythology, but the manner in which Lyra liberates the dead also embodies the spiritual possibilities of fiction. When Lyra tells the Harpy a fantastical version of her own story, the hellish creature screams at her: '*Liar! Liar! Liar!*' The fact that her name is a near homonym of liar is made explicit ('she seemed to be screaming Lyra's name so that *Lyra* and *liar* were one and the same thing', *The Amber Spyglass*, p. 308). Yet, Lyra finds redemption, both for herself and for the dead, by making a bargain with the Harpies who, it is revealed, feed on narrative itself. One of Lyra's companions proposes that the Harpies' new task will be to 'guide the ghosts' of the deceased from the gloom of the dead wastelands to a blissful reunion with creation in exchange for the true stories that the dead have to tell of their lives (*The Amber Spyglass*, p. 334). The idea that a good story signifies salvation seems like a very New Atheist revision – rather than a rejection – of Christian tradition.

In the Land of the Dead, a martyr embraces the opportunity to leave the drab environs (which she describes as neither 'a place of reward or a place of punishment' but as 'a place of nothing'), even if this escape results in personal 'oblivion': 'because it won't be nothing, we'll be alive again in a thousand blades of grass, and a million leaves, we'll be falling in the raindrops and blowing in the fresh breeze, we'll be glittering in the dew under the stars and the moon out there in the physical world which is our true home and always was' (*The Amber Spyglass*, p. 336). This vision is fulfilled when the dead, led back to the living world, dissolve 'into the night, the starlight, the air' (p. 382). Such an ecstatic vision of the organic, cyclical integration of all natural things is pantheistic rather than faithless and, indeed, the narrative's intriguing representation of death is one of the most problematic elements of *His Dark Materials* from a New Atheist perspective. For Pullman, it seems that no one is truly free from divine judgement: instead of the wrath of God – and his mercy – the dead will face the Harpies who will allow spirits to pass into blissful (pantheistic) oblivion only if they can give a good enough account of their lives.

Such an afterlife sounds oddly reminiscent of Christian eschatology, though it is shorn of real redemption: mercy and grace are not part of this account. The Harpies and the dead are locked into an eternal economy of exchange: stories buy peaceful death. It is, ironically, rather less materialist an exchange than that promised by Christianity, since it emphatically does not subscribe to the hope of the resurrection of the body. Although the novel celebrates the tangible and the present, it offers a far more wispily ethereal vision of the future life than the supernatural creed of the Christian religion. Indeed, this version of death, judgement and the afterlife seems no more egalitarian or just than the vision of the afterlife in Lewis's *The Last Battle* (1956). For Lewis, Susan Pevensie appears to have been excluded from heaven because she has grown up, embraced maturity and forgotten Narnia. This shocking twist is one moment cited by Pullman in his *J'accuse*-style condemnation of Lewis in an article for the *Guardian* in 1998 entitled 'The Dark Side of Narnia'. There is no suggestion that Pullman is presenting a literal vision of judgement after death, but it is significant that his allegory relies on punitive concepts derived from Christian eschatological notions of salvation and exclusion. Perhaps Dust itself might be an atomized, quasi-pantheist version of God. If the narrative stresses immanence above and beyond transcendence – the closure of windows between worlds symbolizes the idea that heaven can never be elsewhere and that the present material world is all we have – Pullman's attitude to death suggests that he does not transcend the desire for transcendence. The end of the principal narrative, in which Will and Lyra sacrifice their own romantic happiness for the good of all creation echoes Christian ideas of sacrifice. Naomi Wood draws attention to the fact that, although Pullman's multiverse 'is a narrative world governed by prophecy, a sense of destiny and fate, free will is insisted on, even if it is illusory' ('Paradise Lost and Found', p. 252). In fact, it is another angel – the ancient figure of wisdom, Xaphania – who informs Will and Lyra of their burden and role in saving humanity. So, an irony operates at the end of a narrative which has struggled against divinity: the two young protagonists return to their own worlds to labour for justice, truth and liberty partly because it is the right thing to do, but also because they have been compelled to do so by a quasi-divine (if not omnipotent) being.

Finally, Pullman's narrative excoriates the type of political public religion embodied in the Magisterium, but his trilogy ends with its heroes determined to build something named 'the republic of heaven' (*The Amber Spyglass*, p. 548). It seems that institutional religion is replaced, then, not with a state of pure human freedom but with yet more religion, albeit an ostensibly godless piety. Of course, the language might be republican rather than regal, but the implications are not so very different: how will these brave republicans escape the pragmatic violence of their earlier battles? To our way of thinking,

Rayment-Pickard is right to speculate that Pullman's image of the 'republic of heaven' might just be '"realised eschatology" – that's to say, the kingdom of God by another name' (*The Devil's Account*, p. 87). One of the key questions with which Pullman's narrative engages throughout is how to live ethically in a world where the 'kingdom of God' is an untenable prospect. If the novels wrestle with Jewish and Christian versions of the divine and of revelation, though, they do not offer a radically different alternative of the better society. For Nick Thorpe, writing in a largely sympathetic profile of the author, there is even cause to wonder whether 'in a parallel universe' Pullman 'might have made a good fundamentalist'.[34] Perhaps, though, *His Dark Materials* just *is* that parallel universe: it is, at any rate, utterly dependent on the Judaeo-Christian narrative that it seeks to subvert. In our view, Pullman *re*writes a pre-existing story of fall, exile and redemption without actually transcending the structure of that narrative sequence. All that *His Dark Materials* can do is offer an alternative way of reading that story and though this unorthodox approach is at odds with the doctrines of Roman Catholic and mainline Protestant denominations, it identifies Pullman's trilogy with the wider tradition of Christian heresy rather than as some freestanding, independent story of secular reason or atheism.

To what extent, then, can Pullman's New Atheist novel(s) be found guilty of putting atheist polemic before art? It is possible, ironically enough, to find one line of defence against such an allegation in the work of C. S. Lewis, Pullman's old antagonist. Stranger still, this apologia for the moral tone of *The Amber Spyglass* is to be found in the Christian critic's commentary on the very epic by Milton that inspired Pullman's trilogy. Lewis, in his preface to *Paradise Lost*, reflects that 'when the old poets made some virtue their theme they were not teaching, but adoring, and that what we take for the didactic is often the enchanted' (p. v). One might detect something similar in *His Dark Materials*: the 'didactic' anti-metaphysics, the sermon against piety that becomes particularly intense in *The Amber Spyglass* is perhaps closer to being 'enchanted' than cynical. For Pullman, it also confronts the problems of choice in a world without definitive guidance as to how moral choices might be made. While the narrative seems to enjoy the ethical anarchy of childhood, it ultimately privileges acts of supreme selflessness that are more Christ-like than Satanic: Lyra and Will descend into the land of the dead to find and rescue her murdered friend; they also sacrifice their own personal happiness in order to preserve the universe. Both play a salvific role in a narrative that is ostensibly hostile to the whole notion of salvation, and particularly to vicarious sacrifice. Perhaps, in this sense, Pullman's sensitive description of the emotionally complex end of *Paradise Lost* (Milton's poem 'depends on the interplay between the past and the future, between the regret and hope', he writes) also resonates with the conclusion of his own epic. In the same way that *Paradise Lost* ends with the promise, beyond the garden, of 'many more stories to come', *His Dark Materials* seem to foreshadow many more stories for Will and Lyra in their separate, overlapping worlds (*Paradise Lost*, p. 8).

## CHAPTER FOUR

# SALMAN RUSHDIE AND THE QUARREL
# OVER GOD

In *The Enchantress of Florence* (2008), Salman Rushdie's characteristically exuberant, historically mischievous and theologically
demanding tenth novel, the Emperor Akbar (a character based on
the seventeenth-century Mughal, re-imagined by the novelist as a
secretly sceptical ruler) is exhausted by a private crisis of faith. At
the end of this magic-tinged fable, the Emperor grieves for the loss
of religious toleration. For Akbar, the future will be no harmonious civilization but a place in which people will 'hate their neigh-
bours and smash their places of worship and kill one another once
again in the renewed heat of the great quarrel he had sought to end
for ever, the quarrel over God'.[1] If Rushdie's own work, themati-
cally rich and diverse though it is, has a single, abiding concern it
might be described as 'the quarrel over God'. From *The Ground
Beneath Her Feet* (1999) to *The Enchantress of Florence*; from theologically saturated works of fiction to non-fiction essays which
champion the secular freedom from all forms of religious oppression; from India, through the United Kingdom, all the way to his
third home in the United States of America, this chapter will
explore Salman Rushdie's lifelong exploration of religious conflict.
To what extent does Rushdie's twenty-first-century fiction address
the question of religious belief and disbelief? What impact does the
supposed resurgence of fundamentalisms – of Christian, Islamic
and perhaps even neo-liberal capitalist varieties – have on his more
recent narratives? Why – like all the other New Atheist novelists –
does he esteem the novel *itself* as the front line in the defence of
secular freedoms?

82

# 1

In the last 20 years, Salman Rushdie's novels have (for obvious reasons) been subject to a peculiarly forensic theological critique, his every public utterance seen through the lens of competing religious traditions. On the one hand, many critics regard him as a bold defender of fundamental human freedoms in the teeth of a militant religious threat. On the other, an equally large number of readers – particularly, but by no means exclusively, outside Europe and America – see his writing as a rabidly ideological assault upon their own most cherished values. To be sure, it is difficult to write about Rushdie – despite the best efforts of gossip columnists more interested in the details of his private life – without reference to the *fatwa* that was declared against him on 14 February 1989 by Ayatollah Khomeini of the Islamic Republic of Iran. This spiritually sanctioned death-threat, imposed because Rushdie's fourth novel, *The Satanic Verses* (1988), was regarded as blasphemous in its representation of the Prophet Mohammed, has come to symbolize the rivalry between artistic freedom and religious authority in the modern world.[2] Perhaps, in this respect, we might even see *The Satanic Verses* as the first New Atheist novel.

It is no coincidence, either, that it was a *novel* (and not, say, a work of non-fiction) that generated the international crisis now universally known as the 'Rushdie affair'.

As Graham Ward notes in a sensitive reading of *The Satanic Verses*, the book-burning protests in the UK and the international outrage engendered by its publication, this 'culture war' was at least partly triggered because of the novel's status as 'literature': 'The book's contents were postliberal and postsecular, but its symbolic (and material) value was inseparable from the liberal principle of freedom of speech'.[3] The conflict between 'liberal' and 'theological' values might have been openly acknowledged but, implies Ward, the near-sacred status granted to literature in the West might have been invisible in plain sight. 'The West, the "free world" synonymous with civilization', argues Ward, 'bestows upon certain authors and artists an aura. They are fetishised' (p. 142). What this sociologically inflected reading emphasizes is the ideological complexity of these epoch-making events. High-profile Christian advocates for the novel have been few – indeed, many defenders of free speech are still uncertain how to address the practical issues of religious offence that it provoked – but Rushdie's concerns demand serious evaluation by both people of faith and by those who passionately reject the whole notion of religious adherence.

Any book-length study of religious scepticism in contemporary anglophone fiction would, then, seem to demand focus on Salman Rushdie. Although it would be difficult to overstate the cultural impact of the *fatwa*, in many ways the reaction to *The Satanic Verses* has over-determined the reception of Rushdie's fiction as a whole and, in particular, its attitude to faith. Is his work always a repository of sceptical stories replete with the daring assumption that *nothing* is sacred? Rushdie has distanced himself from some of the rhetoric of New Atheism, while keeping faith with its humanist ideals of freedom of speech.[4] James Wood rightly identifies deracination as a vital element of Rushdie's creative focus.[5] Yet, this perspective also misses something of the extent to which Rushdie's fiction represents a complex set of negotiations with home, religion and nationality. There has been a critical shift in assessments of Rushdie as a purely secular writer, a movement from an emphasis on the novelist who is unreservedly hostile to the religion of his upbringing to a more nuanced view that discerns a complex web of literary representations. Ian Almond, for example, argues that the motif of unconversion and its constellation of 'Enlightenment souls' who see 'through the perceived sham of religion and superstition' in Rushdie's fiction occludes critical recognition that there is 'not one but several Islams in his work, a polyphony of different Islams'.[6] For Almond, writing predominantly about Rushdie's fiction of the 1980s, the 'plethora of different images of Islam' arises from 'a clash of three personae':

> . . . a secular but nevertheless spiritual Rushdie . . . an empirical Rushdie who accepts that the world is all there is . . . and also the Muslim Bombayite, brought up as an insider in a faith he was to step out of, sceptical towards the narrative of Islam but still able to call the Muslim community 'my community' and subscribe to the nascent concept of the 'Secular Muslim'. (p. 96)

In the post-*Satanic Verses* fiction, it is possible to argue that the question of Islam, and of religion more generally, remains equally open-ended and pluralized. Let's begin, then, by counting the Rushdies.

## 2

In an essay entitled 'In Good Faith' (1990) – which appeared two years after the publication of *The Satanic Verses* and in the wake of the extraordinary, violent controversy that ensued – Rushdie reflected that he 'set out to explore, through the process of fiction, the nature of revelation and the power of faith':

> The mystical, revelatory experience is quite clearly a genuine one. This statement poses a problem to the non-believer: if we accept that the mystic, the prophet, is sincerely undergoing some sort of transcendent experience, but we cannot believe in a supernatural world, then *what is going on?*[7]

A key question for all of the writers under review in this book – given their open scepticism – is whether it is possible to write *as if* one believed in the possibility of religious experience as something irreducible to the standard categories available to science and method. However much difficulty and resentment he has encountered, to our eyes Rushdie is arguably more openly committed to the idea that the novelist must attempt a leap of faith than Amis, McEwan or Pullman:

> If one is to attempt honestly to describe reality as it is experienced by religious people, for whom God is no symbol but an everyday fact, then the conventions of what is called realism are quite inadequate. The rationalism of that form comes to seem like a judgement upon, an invalidation of, the religious faith of the characters being described. A form must be created which allows the miraculous and the mundane to co-exist at the same level – as the same order of event. I found this to be essential even though I am not, myself, a religious man. (*Imaginary Homelands*, p. 376)

To what extent, though, is such a fiction of faith possible in the era of instant communication and global commerce? The novel, once a genre celebrated for its imaginative transfigurations of the everyday, struggles to keep pace with the strangeness of real-world narratives shaped by this accelerated culture. One specific challenge faced by Rushdie's internationally oriented literature, which moves with impressive, if alarming, speed between India, Europe and the United

States, is the complexity of representing religious difference while avoiding the temptations of pastiche and parody. Can such novels explore spiritual beliefs without becoming either unwitting religious propaganda or anti-theist polemic?

It is now commonplace to observe that Rushdie's fiction thrives on the interplay between the mystical and the mundane and his plots frequently rotate around an axis that blurs the distinction between the actual and the impossible. *The Enchantress of Florence*, for example, in its blend of dense history, magic realist *jeux d'esprits* and twenty-first-century allegory, celebrates the notion that, in its own words, the 'visionary, revelatory dream-poetry of the quotidian [has] not yet been crushed by blinkered, prosy fact' (*The Enchantress of Florence*, p. 10). Since his first novel, *Grimus* (1975), Rushdie has explored the possibilities of 'speculative fiction' and, in particular, the hinterland between fantasy, fable and realism.[8] *The Ground Beneath Her Feet*, Rushdie's apocalyptic final novel of the twentieth century (and second Christian millennium), emblematizes the collision between faith and rationalism in the polarized world views of two relatively minor characters. 'The true miracle of reason', reflects Sir Darius Xerxes Cama, 'is reason's victory over the miraculous'. Sir Darius's wife, by contrast, is an individual 'for whom the miraculous had long ago supplanted the quotidian as the norm, and who would have been utterly lost, without her angels and devils, in the tragic jungle of the everyday'.[9]

Rushdie roots this – at once very modern and ancient – story of hedonism, creative rivalry and adulation in competing narrative forms. One is a visionary rewriting of the history of rock and roll from its advent in the 1950s to its decadent apotheosis at century's end: in this parallel world, for example, it is Britain, rather than the US that wages war in Vietnam, and Kennedy is not assassinated in Dallas. This kind of virtual history might suggest a worrying capacity for escapism rather than political engagement. Michael Wood, however, argues that the peculiar parallel world constructed in *The Ground Beneath Her Feet* which 'exists at a wide angle to reality' is not simply a sophisticated metafictional game but a speculative mode that demands that its readers reassess 'our damaged reality too'.[10] Indeed, the opening event of the novel is an allusion to this 'damaged' real world: an earthquake that takes the life of Vina Aspara, the female half of a pair of mercurial rock stars whose life is then told in retrospect, takes place on 14 February, 1989, the day on which the *fatwa* against Rushdie was declared. The ground beneath Vina's feet is far from secure just as, the novel suggests, the figurative security of fiction, coupled with the version of secularism that guarantees its freedom, are similarly unstable.

If the novel is buoyed by a fascination with exhilaratingly rebellious and highly commercial twentieth-century pop music, its most explicit narrative source, signalled by an epigram from Rilke's *Sonnets to Orpheus*, is the classical myth of the perfect poet and singer whose journey into the underworld to rescue his wife, Eurydice, is narrated in Ovid's *Metamorphoses*. Ormus Cama, born in Bombay in the late 1930s, is a hybrid figure, combining elements borrowed from the lives of Orpheus, Elvis Presley and John Lennon as well as almost every major pop music icon of the last 50 years. He is also one of literature's most reluctant visionaries, a Wildean apostle of personal liberty, sensualism and the transient who is hijacked by otherworldly waking dreams. Where loss of faith is a trope of Rushdie's early fiction, *The Ground Beneath Her Feet* narrates an unexpected – and deeply reluctant – conversion. Ormus is not only a rock star of vast global fame but a man who has lived his life committed to a belief in the visible without any trace of religious sensibility. Yet he suddenly becomes subject to a terrifying form of visionary experience that ironizes this commitment to the ordinary. For the novel's narrator, Umeed 'Rai' Merchant – a photographer who has known this singer-visionary and his family since childhood – these spiritual intimations are deeply disturbing in their implication that his materialist world view is no longer entirely reliable. 'There is a world other than ours,' Ormus comes to believe, 'and it's bursting through our own continuum's flimsy defenses. If things get much worse the entire fabric of reality could collapse'. Ormus the sceptic suddenly has powerful 'intimations of the end of things' (*The Ground Beneath Her Feet*, p. 347). Even Rai, who describes himself as 'a dyed-in-the-wool unbeliever' acknowledges that this most carnal of poets is 'a true prophet' (p. 351). Although this spiritual transformation is different from a conversion to Christianity or Islam, the event is nevertheless represented as a spectral return of the religious repressed. Significantly, Rai describes the change in his friend (and rival) as 'a kind of revenge of the spirit . . . an irruption, into a life dedicated to the actual and the sensual, of the irrational, the incorporeal. He, who had rejected the unknowable, was being plagued by the unknown' (p. 184). The motif of unexpected epiphany is repeated in *Shalimar the Clown*, when India, a child born of an illicit relationship between Kashmiri and American parents, who, like Ormus, is also committed to the secular and the rational, experiences an ocular 'strangeness . . . the sudden otherness of vision that came and went'.[11] This double-vision testifies to the sensation of duality that is frequently represented as fundamental to the *émigré* experience. However, another implication of Ormus and India's shared, cross-narrative experience is that the line between impiety and religion, irreverence and the sacred is far less well-defined than people who stand either side of it might like to believe.

Rushdie's fiction of the early twenty-first century is particularly sensitive to alternative manifestations of this suspected 'revenge of the spirit'. Indeed, Rai's plaintive query ('What could one trust? How to find moorings, foundations, fixed points, in a broken, altered time?') foreshadows the ontological anxieties of *Fury*, immediate successor to *The Ground Beneath Her Feet* (p. 184). *Fury*, primarily set in the first summer of what the narrator names, with no under-statement, 'the sheer goddamn unbearable head-bursting volume of the third millennium' might be Rushdie's most scathing response to the idea that postmodernity ushers in an era of ethical freedom.[12] The two novels are connected by their sometimes subtle, sometimes overt, use of Greek myth. Where the first is explicitly structured around the story of Orpheus and Eurydice's descent into the under-world, *Fury* is informed by the Roman figures of the Furies (also known as *Erinyes*, in Greek tradition). Malik Solanka, academic manqué, obsessive doll-maker, a man who has been cheated 'of history as well as feeling' and an accidental cult celebrity, is haunted in New York by various women he has spurned or failed who come to represent these incarnations of supernatural vengeance. His comic-erotic adventures notwithstanding (and Malik is one of a variety of ageing Lotharios in Rushdie's work who is a big hit with the opposite sex), Professor Solanka is, like Ormus Cama, confronted by the limits of his own capacity for reason. At one point in the narrative, Solanka feels 'more than ever like a refugee in a small boat, caught between surging tides: reason and unreason, war and peace, the future and the past' (pp. 144–5).

In the case of this formerly mild-mannered Cambridge don, however, it is not visionary experience that terrifies him but his own capacity for violent thought (and, perhaps, deed), that makes him 'conscious of the inexplicable within himself'. This is especially exasperating for a man who has allied himself with 'the prosaic party, the party of reason and science in its original and broadest meaning: *scientia*, knowledge' (p. 128). The novel also makes a playful allusion to Marx's dictum that 'all that is solid melts into air'; in this instance, however, the great materialist thinker's words are used to illuminate not the advent of exchange capital, but the disintegration of reality and the world of stable fact (p. 115). The reason for Solanka's sudden departure for New York is an episode of memory loss in which he suddenly awakes, in a post-drunken daze, standing above his sleeping wife and child with a kitchen knife. Even in his self-imposed exile, he begins to believe that he may be guilty of the serial murders of young female socialites around the city (a fear that proves unfounded). What the novel confronts, however, is the breakdown of reason in a consumerist era in which everything is supposedly understood, easily controlled and ready to be sold:

> . . . even in these microscopically observed and interminably explicated days, what was bubbling inside him defied all explanations. There is that within us, he was being forced to concede, which is capricious and for which the language of explanation is inappropriate. We are made of shadow as well as light, of heat as well as dust. Naturalism, the philosophy of the visible, cannot capture us, for we exceed. (p. 128)

The novel's preoccupation with anger – both the repressed anger of individuals and shared, public rage – is oddly prescient of acts of terror yet to come and the subsequent military response. The book is set in 2000 and was published just days before the terrorist attacks of 9/11. 'This golden age, too, must end . . . as do all such periods in the human chronicle', reflects Solanka (p. 114). He observes that even in an era of reason people are tempted to interpret incidents such as the crash of Concorde in France as a vision in which 'they saw a part of their own dreams of the future, the future in which they too would break through the barriers that held them back, the imaginary future of their own limitlessness, going up in those awful flames' (p. 114). Solanka's own reason is suspended when he reads the world itself as if it were a novel, whose every trivial detail is charged with significance, or more potently still as a myth in which omens are everywhere: he sees a 'great black bird' perched on a rooftop as the Fury, ready to punish him for past transgressions (p. 219). Similarly, after a cathartic acknowledgement of the abuse to which he was subject as a child in Bombay, the narrative emblematizes the relief in the figure of a 'large black crow' that 'drop[s] dead . . . in Gramercy Park. Solanka understood that his own cure . . . was complete. The goddesses of wrath had departed; their hold over him was broken at last' (p. 219). It is similarly tempting to read *Fury* as a vatic text: just as it invokes the Furies of classical literature, we might read Rushdie as a twenty-first-century seer. This would be a mistake but the novel does seem to invite such readings despite its protagonist's hostility, or at least impatience, with the supernatural.

In recent years, Rushdie's fiction, always intrigued by the dynamic, cross-fertilizing potential created by the meetings and mutations of cultural mythologies, has addressed the more problematic consequences of these encounters. *Shalimar the Clown*, in particular, explores the punitive price paid by the world's poorest and most vulnerable citizens when global and local stories are brought into violent contact. The plot, which begins in California in the early 1990s with the murder of a former US ambassador to India, travels across three continents and backwards in time to find the seed of this assassination during the days before and after the Partition of 1947, in Pachigam, a remote, paradise-like village in Kashmir. Like *Fury*, *Shalimar* is charged with a sense of incipient catastrophe: early in the narrative, Nazarébaddor, the village prophetess proclaims that 'The age of prophecy is at an end . . . because what's coming is so terrible that no prophet will have the words to foretell it' (*Shalimar the Clown*, p. 68). The prophet, the seer figure who will be abjured by modernity, curses the world that she will shortly leave. Similarly, Firdaus Noman, mother of the novel's eponymous (and pseudonymous) clown, has fears about her son before he is born (p. 72). Years later, he will commit the murder described in the novel's opening chapter.

A gloomy epigram from *Romeo and Juliet* (Mercutio's curse, from Act III, Scene I, 'A plague on both your houses') is, however, initially subverted by communal tolerance for the illicit erotic relationship between Noman Sher Noman (a.k.a. Shalimar the Clown), a Muslim tightrope walker, and Boonyi Kaul, his feisty lover, a Hindu, and daughter of the village chef and teacher. This 14-year-old Kashmiri version of English drama's most famous tragic lovers, born on the same day to best friends in the Edenic Shalimar gardens, are chastised for indiscreet behaviour but, against convention, marry in dual ceremonies that respect their separate religious backgrounds. Indeed, in a speech proleptic of their weddings (uttered in the days before they were born), Boonyi's mystically inclined father celebrates the unity of their village: 'Who tonight are the Hindus? Who tonight are the Muslims? Here in Kashmir, our stories sit side by side on the same double bill, we eat from the same dishes, we laugh at the same jokes' ( p. 71). In this idealistic world view, no single metanarrative is granted the power to dominate any other, and religious stories, specifically, are allowed to coexist peacefully (or, at the very least, to 'sit side by side'). A delicate harmony achieved by a diverse community (one that also includes a family of Jewish descent alongside Muslims and Hindus) – united by gossip, comic rivalries and complementary folk tales – is wrecked as a result of its contact with a wider world undergoing massive economic and socio-political change. If the novel is disparaging about the bigotry of certain strands of religious fundamentalism, *Shalimar* displays a distinct ambivalence, to say the least, about the liberating claims of the narrative of global capitalism and its impact on the dispossessed. In one striking and much quoted passage, the narrator contemplates the mobility of narrative in an aggressively consumerist epoch:

> Everywhere was now a part of everywhere else. Russia, America, London, Kashmir. Our lives, our stories, flowed into one another's, were no longer our own, individual discrete. This unsettled people. There were collisions and explosions. The world was no longer calm. (p. 37)[13]

Published four years after the terrorist attacks of 9/11, such understated lines quietly suggest that the 'collision' of narratives is not always a cause for celebration. At one level, the Shakesperean allusion embodied by the inter-religious love of Boonyi and Noman signifies the portability of narrative. However, the novel also emphasizes the ethical impact of late capitalism on individual lives and small communities whose stories (personal, religious, folkloric) are not simply restlessly itinerant but subject to endless reinterpretation and exploitation by the powerful. Rushdie's recent fiction displays an acute anxiety about the reckless appropriation of narrative in consumer culture. In *Fury*, for example, Solanka's blithe belief that the 'ransacking of the world's storehouse of old stories and ancient histories was entirely legitimate' is violently undermined when his own other-worldly stories are deployed by a militant faction, in the fictional country of Lilliput-Blefuscu to serve an ultimately sadistic revolution (*Fury*, p. 190).

## 3

For all his sensitivity to the political uses of narrative, Rushdie's treatment of *homo fabulans* – and of the confluence of stories that constitute human history – is not universally regarded as successful. Indeed, in a particularly scathing review of *Shalimar* (titled a lament for the novelist's 'receding talent'), Lee Siegel suggests that from *Midnight's Children* onwards Rushdie has constructed fictional worlds in which all narratives and myths converge, an idea that tempts 'the reader's imagination with the chimera of a universal human destiny resonating out of particular fates'. This view, Siegel suggests, shapes Rushdie's perception of 'reality itself as having been constructed along the lines of *Midnight's Children*' and as a consequence his novels 'insistently annotate and reiterate what he believes to be a priori truths about life'.[14] This view underplays the extent to which Rushdie's use of redemptive, mythic narrative arcs is consistently ironized by plots that are peppered with contingency, accident and human error. However, Siegel is right to emphasize the novelist's enthusiasm for the rag-bag of shared human stories as a kind of spiritual surrogate for orthodox (and authoritarian) religious practice.

Despite its primary historical frame ranging from the 1930s to the late 1990s, Dominic Head identifies *Shalimar* as a distinctively 'post-9/11' novel particularly in the sense that it embodies a 'shifting perception of globalisation'.[15] The seduction and dumping of Boonyi by the charming (and disastrously insouciant) Max Ophuls, the US ambassador to India, might symbolize a particularly dark view of America's global influence, a theme also explored in *The Ground Beneath Her Feet* and *Fury*. Indeed, in the latter novel, Malik Solanka, an émigré who was raised in Bombay, educated at Cambridge and became an improbable media star in London before fleeing to New York – regards the US as 'the great devourer', a creature with an insatiable appetite (*Fury*, p. 69). Solanka, however, is self-consciously willing to be devoured and, in an oddly erotic metaphor, confesses that he has been 'seduced' by the US (p. 87). In one of the novel's plethora of secular prayer-soliloquies to a mythic, godlike US, Solanka invokes one of the country's founding myths. The concept of New England as a 'City on the Hill' was invoked by John Winthrop, first governor of Massachusetts, in his sermon – later known as 'A Model of Christian Charity' (c. 1630) to his fellow Puritan settlers as they set sail for the new world: 'O Dream-America . . . Who demolished the City on the Hill and put in its place a row of electric chairs . . . where everyone, the innocent, the mentally deficient, the guilty, could come to die side by side?' (*Fury*, p. 87). This allusion to Matthew 5. 14 locates Solanka's journey in the overarching American mythology of exodus and the search for a promised land. It also betrays anxieties about the US as a fallen paradise, a dystopia whose global influence is so pervasive that '[e]ven anti-Americanism was Americanism' (p. 87).

Where *Fury* – informed, throughout, by its central protagonist's repressed rage – displays Rushdie's deep ambivalence about the legacy of American ideals of liberty, *Shalimar the Clown*, its immediate successor, pursues these suspicions in more detail. In fact, Andrew Teverson reads *Shalimar* (and, in particular, the relationship between Max and Boonyi) as an allegory of US foreign policy: 'America's power seduces, its affections imprison, its commodities corrupt, and it abandons once it has taken what it wants' (*Salman Rushdie*, p. 219). This view is sustainable – Max is, we are told, 'one of the architects of the postwar world, of its international structures, its agreed economic and diplomatic conventions' as well as, rather improbably, a hero of the French resistance in World War II, a brilliant polymath and, even at 80, a man of extraordinary romantic charm (p. 7). And it is tempting to read Max as a symbol of failed Western liberalism – well-intentioned but frail and greedy – particularly when he is assassinated by the now radicalized Shalimar/Noman. However, the allegorical reading misses Boonyi's sense of agency: she feels trapped by her early marriage and is eager to discover the world beyond the beautiful, tolerant but secluded valley in which she has been raised and decides to pursue the wealthy, powerful American. Although Rushdie is concerned with the potentially malign influence of global economic markets, the novel is equally interested in the contingencies of desire, fulfilled and thwarted. Siegel, for example, suggests that the novel is, in part, a political failure because it elides ideological awareness: Shalimar's radicalization is not truly political but a result of jealousy – a piece of motivation that is at least as old as Shakespeare and something that suggests a humanist sense of tragedy rather than a more dialectical awareness of history.

*Shalimar the Clown* might be accused of romanticizing pre-partition Kashmir – the narrative suggests that the Kashmiri people were 'connected by deeper ties' than those of 'blood or faith' (p. 47) and the valley is consciously troped as a pre-lapsarian Eden – but it also continues Rushdie's career-long wrestling bout with fiction and its capacity to represent theological discourse. The sensitivity of religious communities to their representation in imaginative litera-ture is not something that has escaped Rushdie's notice. Head notes that one legacy of the 'international outcry' about *The Satanic Verses* is that advocates for the validity of the novel now face worldwide scepticism about this most popular of literary forms. After the Rushdie affair, the novel itself 'has come to epitomise a caricatured notion of Western godlessness in the Islamic world (and not just in the minds of Islamists)' (*The State of the Novel*, p. 142). Yet, far from dodging this dispute, Rushdie has remained at the forefront of defending the liberty and integrity of fiction during the 20 years since the *fatwa* was originally proclaimed. In a defence of his own contro-versial novel, entitled 'Is Nothing Sacred?' written at the height of the scandal (and delivered as a lecture by Harold Pinter in 1990 when public appearances by the novelist were impossible), Rushdie coolly observed that 'whereas religion seeks to privilege one language above all others . . . the novel has always been *about* the way in which differ-ent languages, values and narratives quarrel' (*Imaginary Homelands*, p. 419). The word 'quarrel' seems delightfully anachronistic here – a quaint term that might denote a courteous, if heartfelt, disagreement of principle rather than the violent clash of civilizations imaged by the New Atheism. The fact that this is the very word used by Akbar in *The Enchantress of Florence* to describe religious difference does not deny the reality of religiously inflected violence but it does suggest a certain hope, on Rushdie's behalf, that the novel might be a space in which questions about God can be explored without the advent of aggression being taken for granted.

In fact, Rushdie pursued these ideas in a form that was both open and oblique in the immediate successor to *The Satanic Verses. Haroun and the Sea of Stories* (1990), Rushdie's vivid allegory, ostensibly for children (and dedicated to his son, Zafar), might also be his most political defence of the freedom of speech. The novel in many ways anticipates Pullman's experiments with fable, religion and realism in *His Dark Materials*. If Rushdie's tale is muted on the issue of religion, it is voluble about the dangers of totalizing authorities who would attempt to control all language, culture and creativity. The titular hero resists reductive rationalism in his conviction that 'the real world [is] full of magic, so magical worlds could easily be real'.[16] In this fable, rich in linguistic play, Haroun (whose name, like much of the tale, is an allusion to *The Arabian Nights*) embarks on a quest to prevent the great 'sea of stories' from being poisoned by malign, controlling forces. This great ocean becomes an unambiguous metaphor for the alleged power of narrative to challenge totalizing and ossifying modes of interpretation:

> He looked into the water and saw that it was made up of a thousand thousand thousand and one different currents, each one a different colour, weaving in and out of one another like a liquid tapestry of breathtaking complexity; and If explained that these were the Streams of Story, that each coloured strand represented and contained a singe tale . . . And because the stories were held here in fluid form, they retained the ability to change, to become new versions of themselves, to join up with other stories and so become yet other stories; so that unlike a library of books, the Ocean of the Streams of Story was much more than a storeroom of yarns. It was not dead but alive. (*Haroun and the Sea of Stories*, p. 72)

To be sure, Rushdie stops short of sacralizing this living, fluid, unclassifiable sea of narratives. Yet, in didactic passages such as this, *Haroun* valorizes the idea that story itself is somehow singularly worth protecting, particularly from those who would seize any particular text and make their own interpretation definitive and beyond question. 'All these arguments and debates, all that openness, had created powerful bonds of fellowship', notes this fable's narrator (*Haroun and the Sea of Stories*, p. 185). The notion of argument, openness and debate is regarded as something of a liberal totem but all argument requires conversation partners of different understandings, beliefs, theologies and so on. In that sense, Rushdie, unlike some of his contemporaries, is inviting, rather than closing down, the possibility that faith might have a voice in contemporary narrative.

In 'Is Nothing Sacred?' the novelist flirts with the idea that our greatest authors might attain a near holy status. Ultimately, however, he distances himself from such transcendent thoughts: 'I cannot bear the idea of the writer as secular prophet', he concludes (*Imaginary Homelands*, p. 427). Yet, citing Carlos Fuentes's claim that the novel is 'a privileged *arena*', he is clear, like McEwan and Amis, that this literary form has a unique power: the novel, unlike religious discourse, for example, 'does not seek to establish a privileged language, but it insists upon the freedom to portray and analyse the struggle between the different contestants for such privileges' (p. 419). For Rushdie, literature, and the novel in particular, perpetuate imaginative freedoms that are to be regarded as singularly precious (p. 427). This idea recurs in *Shalimar the Clown* in India's struggle to distinguish between religion and imaginative alternatives to the everyday: on the one hand she wants 'to inhabit facts, not dreams' and is dismissive of those she describes as 'True believers, those nightmarish dreamers' who adhere to specific religious creeds (*Shalimar the Clown*, p. 12). The fact that her future career is as a documentary-film maker with a strong political interest emphasizes this investment in the empirical and the rational. However, her desire for 'shadows, chiaroscuro, nuance' and, more importantly, for 'her lost story to be found' suggests a religious sensibility that might find its answers in the narrative security of the novel (p. 12). She does, indeed, discover her own story – or elements of it – though it proves to be one bound up in violence.

Rushdie's recent literary criticism also continues to regard the novel as, in some senses, a special case. In an essay for *The New Yorker*, published in May 2000, as a slightly weary 'Defence of the novel, once again', Rushdie responds to George Steiner's apocalyptic lament for the demise of this great narrative form. This epitaph, argues Rushdie, is not just premature, but is utterly unwarranted as the novel is the very 'hybrid form' for which the critic seems to 'yearn': 'It is part social enquiry, part fantasy, part confessional. It crosses frontiers of knowledge as well as topographical boundaries.'[17] The novelist also suggests that Steiner's recognition that fiction now flourishes primarily in India, Latin America and the Caribbean rather than in the West is 'a very Eurocentric lament' (*Step Across This Line*, p. 56). Outdated imperial anxieties, Rushdie implies, ought not to cloud our recognizing the achievement of a form that is vital, pluralizing and *alive*: 'a new novel is emerging, a post-colonial novel, a de-centred, transnational, inter-lingual, cross-cultural novel' (p. 57). This delighted, almost wide-eyed enthusiasm for the novel appears to stand in relief against the cynicism of some of Rushdie's peers – he cites, in particular, the anxieties of Milan Kundera and Paul Auster – about popular interest and critical engagement with fiction. The 'cultural importance' of 'good literature', Rushdie insists, is not reliant on 'its success in some sort of rating war, but from its success in telling us things about ourselves that we hear from no other quarter' (p. 60). Literature, and the novel in particular, transcends the limits of the everyday – including the excessive rules and regulations of publishing – and speaks to readers, prophet-like, with a unique voice. But how does this voice – one that must pursue true 'intellectual liberty', argues Rushdie, with reference to Orwell – gain such autonomy? And why does he believe that 'what one writer can make in the solitude of one room is something no power can easily destroy' (pp. 59–61)? Whether he intends to or not, this defence of creativity imbues writing with a quasi-transcendental quality, giving fiction, in particular, an aura of eternal durability.

## 4

Does contemporary atheism have a literary language to rival the languages of religious belief? This is, as we have seen, one of the key tenets of the New Atheist novel's own belief system, even if it is one that is rarely borne out in practice. To our eyes, Rushdie's fiction reads as a career-long acknowledgement that new ways of representing the world – grammar, words, strands of imagery – are not easily found. In *Shalimar the Clown*, for example, India, who has no religious faith, fears that the irreligious still lack a mode of imaginative discourse that is not parasitic on sacred vocabularies:

> New images urgently needed to be made. Images for a godless world. Until the language of irreligion caught up with the holy stuff, until there was a sufficient poetry and iconography of godlessness, these sainted echoes would never fade, would retain their problematic power, even over her. (*Shalimar the Clown*, p. 19)

Rushdie's fiction represents a complex set of negotiations with these 'sainted echoes'. His recent fiction has represented religion as a plural phenomenon that might include rich, generous elements (the community in *Shalimar the Clown*, before its exploitation by nationalist and extremist groups, for example) as well as more conservative traditions. He is unique among the authors explored in detail in this study for having been raised in an Islamic, rather than Judeo-Christian, tradition. His own parents were, by his account, faithful if moderate Muslims and he has written with fond respect for his grandfather who he regards as a model of devoted but tolerant commitment to this faith. The novelist has written of his own, apparently sudden and painless, unconversion during his adolescence. In the same essay of spiritual autobiography, 'In God We Trust' (1985; 1990), Rushdie acknowledges the connection between his lack of faith and desire to create: 'But perhaps I write, in part, to fill up that emptied God-chamber with other dreams. Because it is, after all, a room for dreaming in' (*Imaginary Homelands*, p. 377). He writes from a world view of principled atheism and in his non-fiction he has frequently emphasized the moral superiority of ordinary, flawed humanity to the caprices of unpredictable deities. In a letter addressed to 'the Six Billionth World Citizen', for example, originally written for a United Nations anthology of such letters, Rushdie implores the newborn earth-dweller to choose sceptical rationalism rather than the mystical explanations of religion:

> To choose unbelief is to choose mind over dogma, to trust in our humanity instead of all these dangerous divinities. So, how did we get here? Don't look for the answer in 'sacred' storybooks. Imperfect human knowledge may be a bumpy, pot-holed street, but it's the only road to wisdom worth taking.[18]

In the same way, the representation of religion in *Shalimar the Clown* displays a particular contempt for fundamentalism of all kinds – but it also celebrates the possibilities of religious harmony. The advent of fundamentalist Islam in Kashmir, during the mid-1960s, illustrated by the appearance of the preacher with 'beautiful pale eyes that seemed to look right through this world into the next one' (p. 115) is represented as kind of anomaly that need not have thrived. The novel's use of the legend of the 'iron mullahs' is one of Rushdie's most vivid – and terrifying pieces of magic realism:

> The story currently doing the rounds was both military and miraculous. The Indian army had poured military hardware of all kinds into the valley, and scrap metal junkyards sprang up everywhere, scarring the valley's pristine beauty, like small mountain ranges made up of malfunctioning truck exhausts, jammed weaponry and broken tank treads. Then one day by the grace of God the junk began to stir. It came to life and took on human form.

The men who were miraculously born from these rusting war metals, who went out into the valley to preach resistance and revenge, were saints of an entirely new kind. They were the iron mullahs . . . Their breath was hot and smoky, like burning rubber tires, or the exhalations of dragons. They were to be honoured, feared and obeyed. (*Shalimar the Clown*, p. 115)

Despite this avowed scepticism and hostility to the kind of authoritarian supernatural thinking represented by these mythic figures, Rushdie, who has described himself as 'a wholly secular person', may also be the most intensely theological of contemporary British novelists (*Imaginary Homelands*, p. 377). This is not to claim that he is a covert believer or that his fiction subtly subscribes to a theistic world view at which the writer himself candidly baulks. Rather, Rushdie's work remains intrigued by the persistence of belief and the kinds of action that it can generate even as it seeks to challenge both. For Teverson, Rushdie's approach to religion 'is always that of a secular thinker, seeking to understand and interrogate, rather than affirm' (*Salman Rushdie*, p. 73) and this interrogation is, at turns, aggressive and generous.

Perhaps Rushdie comes closest to the views of the New Atheist thinkers in his recent works of non-fiction. In his letter to 'the Six Billionth World Citizen', republished in an anthology of atheism edited by his long-time friend and defender, Christopher Hitchens, the novelist argues that belief in the supernatural is inimical to ethical development:

To my mind religion, even at its most sophisticated, essentially infantilises our ethical selves by setting infallible moral Arbiters and irredeemably immoral Tempters above us: the eternal parents, good and bad, light and dark, of the supernatural realm. ('Imagine There's No Heaven', p. 383)

Such a philosophical rejection of theism is not Rushdie's only grounds for scepticism: a particularly impassioned article on Hindu–Muslim violence in Gujarat, published in March 2002, emphasizes both his Indian heredity and sense of shame regarding recent events. 'If I take pride in India's strengths,' he notes, 'then India's sins must be mine as well' (*Step across This Line*, p. 401). This sense of affective association with India is the calling card that prefaces a blistering attack on the legacy of religious belief and practice. There is neither polite circumlocution in this essay nor is there any attempt to distinguish between alternative strands of belief; instead, Rushdie offers a candidly outraged critique of religion *qua* religion as responsible for such atrocities. He is particularly withering about those who would address religion in what he calls 'the fashionable language of "respect"'. What, demands Rushdie, 'is there to respect in any of this . . . or in any of the crimes now being committed almost daily in religion's dreaded name?' (p. 403). The article concludes with an explicit denunciation of the name he deems responsible for all manner of terror, bloodshed and crime against humanity: 'So India's problem turns out to be the world's problem. What happened in India, happened in God's name. The problem's name is God' (p. 403). The polemical nature of such an article – a response to disgraceful violence, after all – does not lend itself to ambiguity, doubt or qualification. To what extent do Rushdie's novels, though, present the world – and the word 'God' – in such stark terms?

To be sure, the disputed term 'God' contributes to the charged, *fin-de-siècle* mood of *The Ground Beneath Her Feet*. Rai, the novel's sceptical narrator ('the least supernaturally inclined of men'), a photographer who distrusts anything but the evidence of his eyes, tells one European visitor to India that 'hereabouts we are plagued by godness masquerading as goodness'. This 'godness', he suggests, promotes immorality rather than justice: 'The supernatural level is our lifetime detention centre. And every so often our deep spiritualism leads us to massacre one another like wild beasts. Excuse me, but some of us aren't falling for it, some of us are trying to break free into the real' (*The Ground Beneath Her Feet*, p. 223). Later in the narrative he is angrily dismissive of an offhand prayer, offered for his apparently miraculous protection from violence: 'Thank god? No, no, *no*. Let's not invent anything as cruel, vicious, vengeful, intolerant, unloving, immoral and arrogant as god just to explain a stroke of dumb, undeserved luck' (p. 242). Yet Rai, the devout sceptic, recognizes that celebrity culture is, in large part, a response to the 'God-shaped hole' at the heart of a secular, rapaciously capitalist civilization: 'that divine absence which we can fill with our fantasies, becomes the center of our lives' (p. 382).

*Fury*, which also has a sceptical-atheist protagonist, switches its focus from Indian religion to the US culture that dominates the second half of *The Ground Beneath Her Feet*. Echoing the claim that 'God is America's answer to its crisis of identity' made in the essay 'In God We Trust' (*Imaginary Homelands*, p. 391), *Fury* pursues the idea that fundamentalism is not something unique to India. Indeed, a variety of gods are represented as the malaise that afflicts 'the altered states of America' (*Fury*, p. 183). Solanka, an incredulous outsider, is alarmed at the prospect of an escalation of God-talk in American public life: the claim by one vice-presidential hopeful that 'God must move closer to the centre of the country's life' prompts the thought that should 'the Almighty get any closer to the presidency, he'd be living at the end of Pennsylvania Avenue and doing the damn job himself' (p. 183). This light satire of the religious right, however, is not the sole form of religious discourse at play in *Fury*. The novel is also interested in the alternatives to divinity that are generated in a consumerist, postmodern culture characterized by 'disintegrated contemporary reality' (p. 89). The title itself is an appropriation of a classical deity, recycled and reborn on the streets of the metropolis. The 'malevolent Divine' invoked in its title is not the One God of Jewish, Christian or Islamic belief but the *furies* of Greek polytheistic tradition. 'What chance did mortal man have against the devious malice of the gods?' (p. 233). Solanka's ironically neoclassical world view also allows him to see the United States, his new home, the land of exile to which he flees, as a kind of new, geo-political god: 'For a greater deity was all around him: America, in the highest hour of its hybrid, omnivorous power' (p. 44).

The narrative is also fascinated by the culture of simulation that proliferates in contemporary culture in the era of global communication. Solanka's love of the science-fiction genre has a religious dimension: 'In flight from his own life's ugly reality, he found in the fantastic – its parables and allegories, but also its flights of pure invention, its loopy, spiralling conceits – a ceaselessly metamorphosing alternative world in which he felt instinctively at home' (p. 169). His favourite work of fiction, at the age of 20, is explicitly theological: '"The Billion Names of God", in which a Tibetan monastery set up to count the names of the Almighty – believing this to be the only reason for the existence of the universe' (p. 169). This short story brings together sceptical industrialists with a devout, spiritual figure whose views are vindicated. The computer accelerates the search for divine names and the universe comes to an end. Technology is represented in

*Fury* as a species of displaced religion. New media – the internet specifically – creates the experience or the illusion of being godlike:

> Links were electronic now, not narrative. Everything existed at once. This was, Solanka realised, an exact mirror of the divine experience of time. Until the advent of hyperlinks, only God had been able to see simultaneously into past, present and future alike; human beings were imprisoned in the calendar of their days. Now, however, such omniscience was available to all, at the merest click of a mouse. (p. 187)

Professor Solanka, himself a creator of a doll who becomes a cult television hit on a show that features time-travel and encounters with history's great thinkers, notes that cultural amnesia dominates: 'Nobody remembered the original. Everything's a copy, an echo of the past' (p. 142). In such a world, divinity is something that does not disappear but which is manufactured and can turn monstrous. By sculpting his dolls, Solanka himself becomes a parody of the godlike creator, a fact that is not lost on him: 'Clay, of which God, who didn't exist, made man, who did. Such was the paradox of human life: its creator was fictional, but life itself was a fact' (p. 95). This idea takes on a surreal, dangerous guise when Solanka encounters his own likeness in Lilliput-Blefuscu, appropriated for the image of the country's revolutionary leader: 'the creation was real while the creator was the counterfeit! It was as though he were present at the Death of God and the god who had died was himself' (p. 239).

'The Death of God' haunts Rushdie's characters. If the creator/ novelist is confidently sceptical, his characters frequently brood on the paradoxes of belief and unbelief. In the opening pages of *Shalimar the Clown*, for example, India, who has no religious beliefs, is surprised to find herself moved by the story of Santa Monica, named for the weeping mother of Saint Augustine: 'India was contemptuous of religion, her contempt being one of the many proofs that she was not an India. Religion was folly and yet its stories moved her and this was confusing. Would her dead mother, hearing of her godlessness, have wept for her, like a saint?' (*Shalimar the Clown*, p. 18). *The Enchantress of Florence* returns to Rushdie's abiding interest in the relationship between monotheism, power and storytelling. Emperor Akbar, we recall, is publicly religious but privately has severe doubts. Religion, he suspects, is not a matter of truth but a set of practices based on powerful, familial habits that might be displaced when humankind finally usurps the place of God:

> *Maybe there was no true religion.* Yes, he had allowed himself to think this. He wanted to be able to tell someone of his suspicion that men made their gods and not the other way around. He wanted to be able to say, it is man at the centre of things, not God. It is man at the heart and bottom and the top, man at the front and back and side, man the angel and the devil, the miracle and the sin, man and always man, and let us henceforth have no other temples but those dedicated to mankind. This was his most unspeakable ambition: to found the religion of man. (*The Enchantress of Florence*, p. 83)

Such humanist ideas will seem modestly sceptical to an early twenty-first-century liberal audience; to other, more devout readers, how-ever, they might be scandalously impious. Indeed, the Emperor's 'unspeakable ambition' reads like a piece of retrospective prophecy regarding the direction taken by Western culture, at least, a culture which privileges ideas of (a largely godless) progress and the suprem-acy of human (and above all male) achievements. Yet by locating these disbelieving speculations in the mind of a ruler living at the dawn of the modern moment – in the era of the Renaissance in Europe and of expanding trading routes between East and West – the novelist smartly defamiliarizes an issue at the heart of his fiction. Just as Pullman's rewriting of Milton's *Paradise Lost* concludes with the hope that a 'Republic of Heaven' might be built by ordinary mortals, *The Enchantress of Florence* is fascinated by the (im-)possi-bility of godless religion.

## 5

In a very real sense, Akbar's decision to honour the wish of a young ruler whom he has recently slain by building a place of worship that allows, even privileges, argument, encapsulates Rushdie's enduring fascination with the 'quarrel over God'. The slain ruler claims that in Paradise, 'the words *worship* and *argument* mean the same thing' and insists that God is no tyrant. This new house of worship – which the historical Akbar is said to have built – would be 'a house of adora-tion, a place of disputation where everything could be said to every-one by anyone on any subject, including the non-existence of God and the abolition of kings' (*The Enchantress of Florence*, pp. 35–6). Perhaps this temporal 'house of adoration' might be read as an emblem for fiction itself, a true New Atheist novel that can take faith seriously and, at the same time, subject it to serious scrutiny. If Rushdie's fiction suffers when read as a kind of index on world religion – and whose fiction would not? – it has a rare vitality and resourcefulness, together with an aesthetico-political commitment to hybridity, difference and pluralism, that is made richer by its continuing engagement with the 'quarrel over God'. Such utopian spaces as the Emperor Akbar's place of worship are, of course, easy to caricature as the daydream of godless liberalism – but who among us has been tested, persecuted even, as Rushdie has, for robustly defending our own faith?

# CONCLUSION: THE POST-ATHEIST NOVEL

What, in the end, does the New Atheist novel *believe*? It goes without saying that the majority of the novelists and thinkers we have considered in this book would see such a question as the crudest kind of category mistake: atheism is not a belief system, but a form of knowledge, an empiricism, a science. As we argued in the Introduction to this book, however, Richard Dawkins and his fellow New Atheists are not immune to a strange, anti-empirical and deeply mythological piety – towards nature, towards science, towards history and, perhaps most importantly, towards art, beauty and narrative. For us, the New Atheist novel is not just a random accident or the latest publishing trend, but the outworking of this mythopoeic power of the New Atheism itself: the 'story of creation' reaches its logical conclusion in the creation of stories. Such is the only faith the New Atheist finds it impossible to renounce – the faith in story itself. In an almost tautological sense, then, we might say that the New Atheist novel *believes in itself*: it believes in the secular freedom to tell stories, to imagine worlds and to say anything about anything that it – alone – apparently embodies.

## 1

It is just this residual faith in the power of its own fictions that the preceding book has sought to expose. As we have already suggested, there is little if anything that is genuinely 'new' about the New Atheism: this is a distinctly post-Humean but fatally pre-Nietzschean expression of non-belief. Yet, it is also difficult to see how it could be any other way, given that Nietzsche's anti-metaphysical atheism exposes the essentially religious basis of the very scientific critique of religion Dawkins and company seek to promulgate. To Nietzsche's eyes, 'faith in science' is still a *'metaphysical faith'*: 'we godless anti-metaphysicians still take our fire, too, from the flame lit by a faith that is thousands of years old'.[1] If scientific positivism is still metaphysical, it is because it fails to carry out a trans-valuation of the values it attacks: the idols change, to be sure, but everything else remains the same. Perhaps it is also worth recalling here that the people who do not understand what Nietzsche's Madman means when he proclaims that 'God is dead' in the famous scene from *The Gay Science* are not believers, but *atheists*. Just because you don't believe in God, it doesn't follow that you are not religious: Nietzsche's non-believers are, in fact, participating in the popular form of collective worship known as shopping.[2] In the same way, Terry Eagleton argues that secular neo-liberal modernity has presided over – not the final usurpation of the divine – so much as the divinization of the secular: we now speak of 'Nature, Man, Reason, History, Power, Desire' where we used to speak of God (*The Meaning of Life*, pp. 30–1).

According to this line of argument, then, the problem with the New Atheism is that it is not quite atheist *enough*: Dawkins and company buy their non-belief too cheaply – as if just blithely knocking down the infantile bogeyman they call 'God' were enough to have done with religion once and for all. To be sure, the New Atheist novelists do not fall into this trap quite so easily as their philosophico-materialist co-belligerents but it is clear that they, too, find the experience of godlessness to be an exhilarating imaginative and ideological liberation. Whereas Matthew Arnold and the other giants of nineteenth-century literary scepticism famously experienced the death of the Judaeo-Christian God as a terrifying, even bewildering, loss,[3] Amis, McEwan, Pullman and Rushdie depict it as a natural, inevitable and entirely welcome phenomenon that is no more traumatic than disbelief in Zeus, Thor or Father Xmas. One might wonder, though, whether this triumphalism is another example of what, *pace* Dawkins, we might call the 'Atheist Delusion': the illusory belief that, just because you don't believe in God, you are no longer religious. If it is entirely understandable that the New Atheists should not mourn God as fiercely as their predecessors – Chesil Beach is a long way from Dover Beach – it might also be possible to venture a second, more counter-intuitive, explanation: perhaps McEwan and company *have not really undergone the death of God at all.* Perhaps, in other words, the New Atheist novelists are in the same position as Nietzsche's atheist market-dwellers: they have simply traded in one god for another.

For us, then, the New Atheist novel is part of a classically metaphysical, indeed theological story in which science, history, love and art play the same transcendental, redemptive role traditionally assigned to God. It is thus no accident that – like Banquo's ghost – the spectre of religion continually returns to preside over the triumphal atheist feast: God (or at least a fraudulent god) dies in Pullman's *His Dark Materials*, but he is swiftly replaced with a new (and supernaturally ordained) form of transcendence in the inauguration of the Republic of Heaven. As with Pullman, so it is with McEwan, Amis and Rushdie: the critique of religion – whether aesthetic, ethical or political – almost always turns out to be itself religiously inspired. To begin with, Martin Amis and Ian McEwan's *romans à these* in defence of an embattled West are – whether they know it or not – entirely indebted to a long-standing tradition of Christian apocalypticism and Orientalism – what McEwan calls the End of the World Blues. If McEwan and Amis's religion takes the form of a muscular Christian liberalism, Rushdie and Pullman are less confident about the rightness of their own values and more generous to other ways of narrating existence. Both affirm a non-supernatural spirituality that might not be recognized by conservative Christian, Jews, Muslims or Hindus but, which nevertheless, affords a place for the ineffable, the sublime and that which lies beyond the purview of human understanding. Perhaps what unites all four novelists, though, is a kind of neo-Romantic belief in the potential of art – and particularly fiction – to replace a now untenable faith in the divine: Amis, McEwan, Pullman and Rushdie all valorize a free utopian space called the novel in which it is possible for anything and everything to be thought and said. In the end, the New Atheist novel stands or falls on whether its readership can share this faith in the saving power of fiction itself. Can the humble work of fiction carry the enormous weight the New Atheist novelists place upon it? Is the contemporary Western novel really the embodiment of free speech, tolerance and pluralism – as they claim – or just one more bully pulpit for neo-liberal hegemony? Why should anyone – let alone an atheist – believe that only literature can save us now?

2

What other – perhaps more fertile – ways might there be to narrate the relationship between theism and atheism, faith and doubt, the sacred and the secular? After all, it is not as if religious doubt is a new phenomenon in literary fiction. One would have a quicker job listing those writers who have a straightforward, uncritical faith than constructing a canon of sceptics and theological outcasts. For the critic and novelist James Wood, this may be because writing and reading fiction offers an experience of *sceptical* belief that is analogous (but superior) to the state of pious devotion:

> Once religion has revealed itself to you, you are never free. In fiction, by contrast, one is always free to choose not to believe, and this very freedom, this shadow of doubt, is what helps to constitute fiction's reality. Furthermore, even when one is believing fiction one is 'not quite' believing, one is believing 'as if'. . . Fiction asks us to judge its reality; religion asserts its reality. And this is all a way of saying that fiction is a special realm of freedom.[4]

If Wood still affirms the 'special realm of freedom' that is literature over and against the iron grip of religious belief, it is striking that the novel never becomes a surrogate religion that demands absolute devotion in the polemical manner of the New Atheist novel. In Wood's account, the 'true secularism of fiction' resides – not in a superior claim to describe the real – but in the fact that it 'moves *in the shadow of doubt*, knows itself to be a true lie, knows that at any moment it might fail to make its case' (*The Broken Estate*, pp. xiv–xv).

Yet, even this attenuated faith in the secular power of fiction is interestingly tested by Wood's own deeply theological first novel, *The Book against God* (2003). To Wood's wayward narrator Thomas Bunting, the titular 'book' is a kind of never-ending work in progress designed to disprove, once and for all, the existence of the Judaeo-Christian God. Bunting – an accomplished liar, apathetic doctoral student and angry non-believer – obsessively compiles notebooks full of quotations from the theological and philosophical canon that extend the cause of atheism. One friend, Max, suggests that Thomas's whole project is, in fact, a covert prayer with God his 'intended reader'; responding to Thomas's claim not to believe in the deity, Max gently but firmly insists: 'Yes you do . . . Yes you do'.[5] For Wood, it is clear that Thomas – whose Christian name embodies his own proclivity for doubt – is haunted by the faith he desperately, if secretly, tries to disprove. Perhaps we might even see *The Book against God* as a re-telling of the parable of the Prodigal Son and an Oedipal tale of wrestling with parental authority: Thomas's father, Peter, is like his apostolic forefather, a rock of the Church. In a deeper sense, Wood's novel is also emblematic of the anglophone novel's self-conscious struggle with its biblical heritage: the New Atheist novel is merely the latest chapter in the impossible, unfinishable Book against God.

For us, the contemporary novel – both within and without the UK – may more profitably be described as a kind of 'post-atheist fiction': what it dramatizes is neither a return to some pre-rational religious dogmatism nor the fetishization of liberal enlightenment values but an attempt to move beyond the Manichean clash of religious and secular fundamentalisms epitomized by 9/11 and its aftermath. It is revealing, perhaps, that the New Atheist novelists discussed in this book are all British – although Rushdie was raised in India and now lives in the United States of America – and their upbringing may well contribute to the somewhat insular, defensive and paranoid world view of works like *Saturday*. At the same time, however, a younger generation of British writers like Hanif Kureishi, Monica Ali and Zadie Smith are now offering more complex and variegated pictures of the multi-cultural, multi-faith world beyond Henry Perowne's Georgian sash window. To range more widely, contemporary British novelists as different as Nick Hornby, Jim Crace and David Mitchell have all produced fictions that test the moral capacities of humanity in an era 'after God' without ever being mistaken for religious confessors. One can also find vastly more curious portraits of the relationship between religious fundamentalism and secularism than anything offered by Amis and McEwan in the work of such figures as Naguib Mafouz, Nawal El Saadawi (Egypt), Haidar Haidar (Syria), Rachid al-Daif (Lebanon), Turki al-Hamad (Saudi Arabia) and Orhan Pamuk (Turkey). Perhaps one of the most fertile breeding grounds for post-atheist fiction, though, might be North America: John D. McClure has identified Don DeLillo, Louise Erdrich, Toni Morrison and Thomas Pynchon as novelists whose work tells 'stories about new forms of religiously inflected seeing and being'. Such stories are 'dramatically partial and open-ended' and 'do not promise anything like full redemption', McClure contends, but arguably they do something much smaller and more important that, for all its grandiose claims to freedom, tolerance and empathy, the New Atheist novel is never able to credibly accomplish: they show us what it is really like to believe in God.[6]

Finally, of course, we should recall that it is often religious novelists – rather than atheists – who offer the most compelling imaginative depictions of non-belief, precisely because they know what it means to have believed in the first place. To be sure, the late John Updike was rare among great twentieth-century novelists as a confessing (if not pietistic) Christian, but he could also write more powerfully than Amis, McEwan or Pullman on the failure of belief. Updike's *In the Beauty of the Lilies* (1997) – a vast domestic saga that follows the 'American century' via the life of one family and their relationship with the gods of Christianity and Hollywood – begins with a clergyman losing his faith. By the same token, *Seek My Face* (2002) is structured around the reminiscences of a 70-something painter, Hope Chafetz, who has become consumed with spiritual scepticism: '*For a long time I have lived as a recluse, fearing the many evidences of God's non-existence with which the world abounds.*'[7] For Ian McEwan, who published a generous tribute to Updike just a few days after the American writer's death in 2009, Updike's skill as a novelist of the particular was, in fact, intimately connected with his religious beliefs. Such 'religious seriousness', McEwan argues, is what enables Updike to create an atmosphere of metaphysical panic in a short story called 'The Wallet' (1984) without ever directly invoking God:

> [I]t is unlikely that an atheist could have conjured so much from the minor domestic disturbance that follows . . . Like much that appears secular in Updike, this story is suffused with his religious seriousness.[8]

If this acknowledgement of Updike's religion is not surprising – given that it was such a public part of his identity as a novelist – what is much less predictable and more welcome here is McEwan's recognition that the writer's aesthetic success was inextricably welded to his religious faith. In the end, this might be the simplest and most powerful artistic argument against the New Atheist novel and it is made by one of its chief exponents: a world without God would also be a world without John Updike.[9]

## 3

What, to bring this book to a close, does the future hold for the New Atheist novel? It goes without saying that neither religious nor atheist fundamentalisms are going away any time soon. On the contrary, they feed off one another symbiotically: Richard Dawkins is today an invaluable recruiting sergeant for US Christian fundamentalists in their ongoing culture war against godless, decadent liberalism. To make our own stance absolutely clear, Martin Amis, Ian McEwan, Philip Pullman and Salman Rushdie are right to challenge religion if and when it inspires anti-rationalism, misogyny, racism and terrorism. However, this book has tried to argue that their fictions are by no means immune to the very irrationalism, intolerance and ignorance they seek to contest. For all its claims to occupy a free, open and rational space where anything can be thought and said, the New Atheist novel frequently resembles nothing so much as an aesthetico-political echo chamber in which the same shrill voices reverberate louder and louder. Just like their philosophical and scientific comrades, Amis, McEwan, Pullman and Rushdie too often end up bearing witness to the sheer poverty of our public discourse on religion at a time when caution, sensitivity and discrimination have never been more necessary. If a new rational critique of religious extremism is to be mounted – and it is certainly needed – it must go hand in hand with an equally rigorous interrogation of its own closed circle of political, cultural and indeed *religious* assumptions. So, can the New Atheist novel face up to its own limits, equivocations and ideological blind spots and finally become the free, open and above all self-critical space it has always claimed to be? Perhaps, once again, we must have faith.

# NOTES

## INTRODUCTION: THE NEW ATHEIST NOVEL

[1] Sam Harris, *The End of Faith: Religion, Terror and the Future of Reason* (New York: W. W. Norton, 2004); Daniel C. Dennett, *Breaking the Spell: Religion as a Natural Phenomenon* (London: Allen Lane, 2006); Richard Dawkins, *The God Delusion* (London: Transworld, 2nd edition 2007) and Christopher Hitchens, *God is Not Great: The Case against Religion* (London: Atlantic Books, 2007). See also Michel Onfray, *Traité d'athéologie: Physique de la métaphysique*, Paris, Grasset, (2005), trans. by Jeremy Leggatt as *Atheist Manifesto: The Case against Christianity, Judaism, and Islam* (New York: Arcade, 2007); A. C. Grayling, *Against All Gods: Six Polemics on Religion and an Essay on Kindness* (London: Oberon, 2007) and Sam Harris, *Letter to a Christian Nation: A Challenge to the Faith of America* (London: Bantam, 2007). All further references will be given in the text.

[2] It is, in fact, now possible to detect something of a theological counter-reformation: Terry Eagleton, 'Lunging, Flailing, Mispunching', *London Review of Books*, 19 October 2006; Alastair McGrath and Joanna Collicutt McGrath, *The Dawkins Delusion? Atheist Fundamentalism and the Denial of the Divine* (London: SPCK, 2007); Tina Beattie, *The New Atheists: The Twilight of Reason and the War on Religion* (London: Darton, Longman & Todd, 2007); John Cornwell, *Darwin's Angel: A Seraphic Response to The God Delusion* (London: Profile 2007).

[3] John Gray, *Black Mass: Apocalyptic Religion and the Death of Utopia* (London: Allen Lane, 2007), p. 189. All further references will be given in the text.

[4] To be sure, the New Atheists do not make any particular claim for their own novelty. It remains the case, though, that their thought is almost cryogenically suspended in the early nineteenth century as if philosophy came to an end somewhere after Hume. In a 500-page anthology of atheist literature through the ages, for instance, Christopher Hitchens is perversely unable to find any room for Nietzsche.

[5] Richard Dawkins, *The Selfish Gene* (Oxford: Oxford University Press, 1989 [1976]).

[6] See RichardDawkins.Net (http://richarddawkins.net); Sam Harris's website (www.samharris.org/); The New Atheism (http://newatheism.org); The Brights' Net (www.the-brights.net); The Rational Response Squad

(www.rational responders.com) and Nontheism (http://nontheism.org) among many other websites.

[7] Craig Unger, *The Fall of the House of Bush: The Delusions of the Neo-Conservatives and American Armageddon* (London: Pocket, 2008). For Christian Zionists, the return of the Jews to the Holy Land and the establishment of the State of Israel are in accordance with Biblical prophecy and, thus, a prerequisite for the second coming of Christ. In political terms, this leads them to adopt a strong pro-Zionist position even though their real theological goal is totally at odds with Judaism.

[8] As Harris himself is forced to admit, the Qur'an depicts the 'greater' *Jihad* as an internal struggle through which the believer seeks to overcome his or her own sinfulness (*End of Faith*, p. 111). In the case of the 'lesser' *Jihad* – the holy war – the Prophet depicts it as by no means a permanent act of war but a defensive and preventative measure that should only be undertaken under particular circumstances: 'Fight in the way of Allah against those who fight you, but begin not hostilities. Lo! Allah loves not aggressors' (02:190). See Rudolph Peters, *Jihad in Classical and Modern Islam: A Reader*, 2nd ed. (Princeton, NJ: Markus Wiener Publishers, 2005), p. 116.

[9] However, the religious explanation for suicide bombings once again runs entirely contrary to the available evidence, as compiled by Robert Pape in the single most important study of the phenomenon. According to Pape – who has analysed every known case of suicide attacks from 1980 to 2005 (some 315 attacks as part of 18 campaigns) – there is little connection between suicide terrorism and Islamic fundamentalism. To Pape's eyes, what nearly all suicide terrorist attacks have in common is a specific secular goal: to compel modern democracies to withdraw military forces from territory that the terrorists consider to be their homeland. While the New Atheists claim that their own explanation of suicide bombings is based on the literal meaning of what the bombers themselves actually say – '*these people believe what they say they believe*' (*God Delusion*, p. 345) – they systematically ignore or downplay the explicit political justifications the bombers give for their actions. For Harris, any such explicit political goal 'does not in the least suggest that they are not primarily motivated by their religious dogmas' (*End of Faith*, pp. 250–1). In their own videotaped statements, however, the British 7/7 bombers explicitly state that their attacks are a response to the British government's support for the Iraq war. Perhaps, though, they didn't really believe what they said they believed. See Robert Pape, *Dying to Win: The Strategic Logic of Suicide Terrorism* (New York: Random House, 2005).

[10] Alan Dershowitz, *The Case for Israel* (Hoboken, NJ: John Wiley, 2003), p. 2. Quoted by Harris, *The End of Faith*, p. 135. In Harris's work, the strongly pro-Israel activist Dershowitz is bizarrely cited as an objective witness to the rights and wrongs of the Israel/Palestine conflict.

[11] Immanuel Kant, 'An Answer to the Question: What is Enlightenment?', in *Kant's Political Writings*, trans. by H. B. Nisbet and ed. by Hans Reiss (Cambridge: Cambridge University Press, 1970), pp. 54–60.

[12] Mary Midgely, *Evolution as a Religion: Strange Hopes and Stranger Fears* (London and New York: Routledge, 2002), pp. 1, 34.

13 Theodore Dalrymple, 'What the New Atheists Don't See', *City Journal*, Autumn 2007 (www.city-journal.org/html/17_4_oh_to_be.html) (5 January 2009).

14 See Andrew Ross, *The Chicago Gangster Theory of Life* (London: Verso, 1994); N. Katherine Hayles, *How We Became Posthuman: Virtual Bodies in Cybernetics, Literature and Informatics* (Chicago: University of Chicago Press, 1999); Tiziana Terranova, *Network Culture: Politics for the Information Age* (London: Pluto, 2004). In Hayles's account, *The Selfish Gene* is 'deeply informed by anthropomorphic constructions': Dawkins's rhetoric 'attributes to genes human agency and intention, creating a narrative of human struggle for lineage [which] overlays onto the genes the strategies, emotions and outcomes that properly belong to the human domain', pp. 227–8.

15 Matt Ridley, 'Richard Dawkins and the Golden Pen', in *Richard Dawkins: How a Scientist Changed the Way We Think*, ed. by Alan Grafen and Mark Ridley (Oxford: Oxford University Press, 2007), pp. 265–9.

16 Charles Darwin, *The Origin of Species* (New York: Gramercy Books, 1979 [1859]), p. 459.

17 Richard Dawkins, *Unweaving the Rainbow: Science, Delusion and the Appetite for Wonder* (London: Allen Lane/The Penguin Press, 1998), blurb.

18 Christopher Hitchens, 'Introduction' to *The Portable Atheist: Essential Readings for the Non-Believer*, ed. by Christopher Hitchens (London: Da Capo Press, 2007), pp. xiii–xxvi, p. xxiv. All further references will be given in the text.

19 Georg Lukács, *Theory of the Novel: A Historico-Philosophical Essay in the Forms of Great Epic Literature*, trans. by A. Bostock (Cambridge, MA: MIT, 1971).

20 Ian McEwan, 'Only Love then Oblivion: Love Was All They Had to Set against Their Murderers', *Guardian*, 15 September 2001 (www.guardian.co.uk/world/2001/sep/15/september11.politicsphilosophyandsociety2).

21 Salman Rushdie, *Imaginary Homelands: Essays and Criticism, 1981–1991* (London: Granta, 1992), p. 377.

22 Salman Rushdie, *The Enchantress of Florence* (London: Jonathan Cape, 2008), pp. 35–6.

23 Martin Amis, 'Terror and Boredom: The Dependent Mind', in *The Second Plane: September 11: 2001–2007* (London: Jonathan Cape, 2008), pp. 47–94, p. 79. In Amis's words, 'The stout self-sufficiency or, if you prefer, the extreme incuriosity of Islamic culture has been much remarked'.

## CHAPTER ONE: IAN McEWAN'S END OF THE WORLD BLUES

1 Ian McEwan, 'Move Over, Darwin', *Guardian*, 20 September 1998; 'A Parallel Tradition', *Guardian*, 1 April 2006; 'Ian McEwan: I hang on to hope in a tide of fear', *Independent*, 7 April 2007; 'The TNR Q & A: Ian McEwan on Bellow, the Internet, Atheism, and Why His Books Are Still Scary', *New Republic*, 11 January 2008. All further references will be given in the text.

[2] Ian McEwan, 'End of the World Blues', in *The Portable Atheist: Essential Readings for the Non-Believer*, ed. by Christopher Hitchens (London: Da Capo Press, 2007), pp. 351–65, p. 352. All further references will be given in the text.

[3] Ian McEwan, *Black Dogs* (London: Vintage, 1992), p. 19. All further references will be given in the text.

[4] James Wood, 'Why It All Adds Up' (Review of *Enduring Love*), *Guardian*, 4 December 1997, pp. 9–10. In Woods' polemical view, McEwan's excessively schematic works are 'efficient fictional engines, but not true novels'.

[5] Ian McEwan, *Enduring Love* (London: Vintage, 1997), p. 48. All further references will be given in the text.

[6] Dominic Head, *Ian McEwan*, Contemporary British Novelists (Manchester: Manchester University Press, 2007). In Head's view, McEwan's fiction exposes systematic explanations of the world as 'limited or damaging', but it also shows the absence of such systems to be simply catastrophic: we have 'nothing against which the self can be measured or defined' without them, p. 16.

[7] As Roger Clark and Andy Gordon note, one of the obvious cultural contexts for *Enduring Love* is Alan Sokal and Jean Bricmont's notorious attempts to expose what they saw as the intellectual charlatanism of continental philosophy's (again, alleged) attempts to reduce science to just another narrative construction or story. In a sense, we could read the conclusion of *Enduring Love* as a kind of inverted version of the Sokal hoax in *Social Text* which seeks to prove just how indebted science is to narrative form: McEwan's entirely fictional case study was apparently submitted for publication to the *Psychiatric Bulletin* and it did manage to fool many reviewers of the novel. See Roger Clark and Andy Gordon, *Ian McEwan's 'Enduring Love'* (London: Continuum, 2003), pp. 68–9.

[8] Theo Tait, 'A Rational Diagnosis' (Review of *Saturday*), *Times Literary Supplement*, 11 February 2005, pp. 21–2, p. 22.

[9] Ian McEwan, 'Only Love Then Oblivion. All further references will be given in the text. (www.guardian.co.uk/world/2001/sep/15/september11.politicsphilosophyandsociety2)

[10] James Wood, 'On a Darkling Plain: Ian McEwan's *Saturday*', *The New Republic*, 14 April 2005. All further references will be given in the text.

[11] Ian McEwan, Author Interview, Random House Readers' Group Reading Guides (www.randomhouse.co.uk/readersgroup/readingguide.htm?command=Search&db=/catalog/main.txt&eqisbndata=0099429799#interview) (1 May 2008).

[12] Ian McEwan, *Atonement* (London: Vintage, 2002), p. 36. All further references will be given in the text.

[13] Ian McEwan, *Saturday* (London: Vintage, 2006), p. 38. All further references will be given in the text.

[14] However, as we were in the process of writing this chapter, McEwan put on record his hatred of what he calls 'Islamism'. In a June 2008 interview, he said: 'I myself despise Islamism [lo disprezzo], because it wants to create a society that I detest, based on religious belief, on a text, on lack of freedom for women, intolerance towards homosexuality and so on',

'McEwan et L'Islamismo: "Lo disprezzo"', *Corriere della Sera*, 21 June 2008. Our translation.

15 For Bernard Lewis, Islamic culture from the sixteenth to the nineteenth centuries suffered from a fatal lack of curiosity about Europe in contrast to the European 'Orientalist' interest in Islam. In recent years, however, this thesis has been decisively challenged by archival scholars who have uncovered the wealth of literature about Europe contained in Islamic libraries. See, for example, *In the Lands of the Christians: Arabic Travel Writing in the Seventeenth Century* ed. by Nabil Matar (London: Routledge, 2003).

16 Christopher Hitchens, 'On the Frontiers of Apocalypse', in *Love, Poverty and War: Journeys and Essays* (London: Atlantic, 2005). In his voluminous writings of the subject, Hitchens consistently repeats – without ever justifying – the view that Islamism is the product of 'self-righteousness, self-pity and self-hatred'.

17 In *Saturday*, Henry describes reading a novel in which 'One visionary saw through a pub window his parents as they had been some weeks after his conception, discussing the possibility of aborting him' (p. 66). This is a scene from McEwan's own *The Child in Time* (London: Vintage, 1997).

18 Ian McEwan, *On Chesil Beach* (London: Jonathan Cape, 2007). All further references will be given in the text.

## CHAPTER TWO: MARTIN AMIS AND THE WAR FOR CLICHÉ

1 Martin Amis, 'The Voice of the Lonely Crowd', in *The Second Plane: September 11: 2001–2007* (London: Jonathan Cape, 2008), pp. 11–20, p. 15. In addition to non-fiction writings, this collection contains 2 short stories, 'In the Palace of the End' and 'The Last Days of Mohammed Atta', and a description of an abandoned novella called 'The Unknown Known'. All further references will be given in the text.

2 Martin Amis, 'The Amis Papers', *Observer*, October 1, 2006; '30 Things I've Learned about Terror', *Independent*, 8 October 2006; 'Martin Amis: You Ask the Questions', *Independent*, 15 January, 2007 and 'The Two Faces of Amis', *Independent*, 29 January 2008. In *The Second Plane*, the work of Harris and Hitchens are alluded to throughout the text.

3 Martin Amis, *The War against Cliché: Essays and Reviews 1971–2000* (London: Jonathan Cape, 2001), p. xv. All further references will be given in the text.

4 It is striking how traditional, indeed parochial, is Amis's own perspective for a literary critic who came of age during the theoretical revolutions of the 1970s and 1980s. Apart from the occasional sniffy allusion to the 'gurus and yogis of structuralism' (*The War against Cliché*, p. 76), the novelist's main reference points remain the canonical figures of pre-war English literary criticism (Bloomsbury, Leavis, Richards, Empson, Wimsatt, Trilling, Wilson Knight and Frye) and his contempt for the professional critics of modern academia is marked (pp. xii–xiii). In Amis's view, the only contemporary literary critic of note seems to be the decidedly un-contemporary James Wood.

[5] M. Hunter Hayes, 'A Reluctant Leavisite: Martin Amis's "Higher Journalism"', in *Martin Amis: Postmodernism and Beyond*, ed. by Gavin Keulks (Basingstoke: Palgrave Macmillan, 2006), pp. 197–210. In *The War against Cliché*, Amis includes a section with the very Leavisite title of 'Great Books' and declares Saul Bellow's *The Adventures of Augie March* to be the Great American Novel: 'Search no further' (p. 447).

[6] Paul Ricoeur, *Memory, History, Forgetting*, trans. by Kathleen Blamey & David Pellauer (Chicago: University of Chicago Press, 2006), p. 82. In Ricoeur's words, 'The ideological process is opaque in two ways. First, it remains hidden; unlike utopia, it is unacknowledged; it masks itself by inverting itself, denouncing its adversaries in the field of competition between ideologies, for it is always the other who stoops to ideology.' Thanks to Alex Paknadel for supplying this reference.

[7] Samuel P. Huntington, *The Clash of Civilisations and the Remaking of World Order* (New York: Simon & Schuster, 1988).

[8] Ziauddin Sardar, 'Welcome to Planet Blitcon', *New Statesman*, 11 December 2006. In Sardar's article, 'Blitcon' is an abbreviation of 'British literary neo-conservatism'.

[9] Marjorie Perloff, 'Martin Amis and the Boredom of Terror' (Review of *The Second Plane*), *Times Literary Supplement*, February 13, 2008.

[10] Martin Amis, 'The Voice of Experience', interview, *The Times*, 9 September 2006. To quote Amis's own words: 'What can we do to raise the price of [Islamist terrorists] doing this? There's a definite urge – don't you have it? – to say, "The Muslim community will have to suffer until it gets its house in order". What sort of suffering? Not letting them travel. Deportation – further down the road. Curtailing of freedoms. Strip-searching people who look like they're from the Middle East or from Pakistan . . . Discriminatory stuff, until it hurts the whole community and they start getting tough with their children'. For Terry Eagleton, writing in the introduction to a new edition of his book *Ideology*, Amis's remarks were comparable to 'the ramblings of a British National Party thug', *Ideology: An Introduction* (London: Verso, 2nd edition, 2007). In a letter written to the *Guardian* in his own defence, Amis has stressed that his comments were merely a heat-of-the-moment reaction following the revelation of an Islamist plot to blow up 10 transatlantic airliners, *Guardian*, 12 October 2007.

[11] However, it is revealing that Amis does not accept the equivalent distinction between Zionism and Judaism: it is perfectly possible to be anti-Islamist without being anti-Islam but critics of Zionism are always vulnerable to the suspicion of anti-Semitism. In a 2008 interview with the *Independent*, for instance, Amis describes the motivation of the pro-Palestinian British Left in precisely these terms: 'I know we're supposed to be grown up about it and not fling around accusations of anti-Semitism, but I don't see any other explanation. It's a secularised anti-Semitism', 'The Two Faces of Amis'.

[12] To our eyes, the French political scientist Olivier Roy is the most reliable contemporary guide to the disparate web of groups, interests and forces that go under the name of 'Islamism'. For Roy, it is crucial to distinguish between

political Islamism – which he defines as the attempt to build an Islamic state – and post-Islamist Neo-Fundamentalism – which is a globalized militancy that exists independently of any national political programme: Islamist movements would thus include the Iranian Islamic revolution, Palestine's Hamas, Algeria's FIS, Lebanon's Hizbullah, the Turkish Refah Partisi and the Muslim Brotherhood in Egypt whereas the paradigm for Neo-Fundamentalism would be al-Qaeda. In Roy's account, more generally, al-Qaeda is less the irrational and retrogressive cult imagined by Amis and more a thoroughly postmodern, de-territorialized phenomenon. See Olivier Roy, *Globalised Islam: The Search for a New Umma* (London: Hurst, 2004).

[13] See also Martin Amis, 'The Voice of Experience': 'the only thing the Islamists like about modernity is modern weapons. And they're going to get better and better at that. They're also gaining on us demographically at a huge rate. A quarter of humanity now and by 2025 they'll be a third. Italy's down to 1.1 child per woman. We're just going to be outnumbered'. In this interview, as in the published work, the distinction between Islam and Islamism simply disappears: all Muslims, it seems, are natural born Islamists.

[14] Jean Paulhan, *The Flowers of Tarbes, or Terror in Literature*, trans. by Michael Syrotinski (Chicago: Illinois University Press, 2006 [1936]), p. 24. All further references will be given in the text. In many ways, the parallel between the artist and terrorist in post-Romantic aesthetics has itself become something of a cliché in recent criticism: see, for example, Margaret Scanlan, *Plotting Terror: Novelists and Terrorists in Contemporary Fiction* (Charlottesville: University of Virginia Press, 2001); Alex Houen, *Terrorism and Modern Literature: From Joseph Conrad to Ciaran Carson* (Oxford: Oxford University Press, 2002); Frank Lentricchia and Jody McAuliffe, *Crimes of Art + Terror* (Chicago and London: University of Chicago Press, 2003).

[15] Tibor Fischer, 'A Tour of Stalin's Labour Camps' (Review of *House of Meetings*), *Daily Telegraph*, 11 October 2006. In Fischer's somewhat more ungenerous view, Amis has become 'an atrocity-chaser . . . now constantly on the prowl for gravitas-enlargement offers (the Holocaust, serial killers, 9/11, the Gulag, the Beslan siege) as if writing about really bad things will make him a really great novelist'.

[16] For many other critics, September 11 was also clearly a symbolic, aesthetic or rhetorical event. See Paul Virilio, *Ground Zero*, trans. by Chris Turner (London: Verso, 2002); Jean Baudrillard, *The Spirit of Terrorism and Requiem for the Twin Towers*, trans. by Chris Turner (London: Verso, 2002); Geoffrey Galt Harpham, 'Symbolic Terror', *Critical Inquiry* 28 (Winter 2002), pp. 573–9; Slavoj Žižek, *Welcome to the Desert of the Real* (London: Verso, 2003); John Frow, 'The Uses of Terror and the Limits of Cultural Studies', *Symploke* 11, 1–2 (2003), pp. 69–76; Homi K. Bhabha, 'Terror and After . . .' *Parallax* 1 (2002): pp. 3–4 and Jacques Derrida and Giovanna Borradori, 'Autoimmunity: Real and Symbolic Suicides', in *Philosophy in a Time of Terror: Dialogues with Jacques Derrida and Jurgen Habermas*, ed. by Giovanna Borradori (Chicago: University of Chicago Press, 2003), pp. 85–136. In our view, though, the prize for the most

immediate such response goes to Karlheinz Stockhausen speaking to journalists on 16 September 2001: ' Well, what happened there is, of course — now all of you must adjust your brains — the biggest work of art there has ever been', Karlheinz Stockhausen, 'Huuuh! Das Pressegespräch am 16. September 2001 im Senatszimmer des Hotel Atlantic in Hamburg', *MusikTexte* 91 (2002), pp. 69–77, p. 76, our translation.

[17] R. W. Southern, *Western Views of Islam in the Middle Ages* (Cambridge, MA: Harvard University Press, 1965), p. 105. See Ian Almond, *The New Orientalists: Postmodern Representations of Islam from Foucault to Baudrillard* (London: IB Tauris, 2007) for an examination of this recurring trope within contemporary fiction and theory.

[18] This 'apocalyptic-epiphanic' (*War against Cliché*, p. 182) streak is present throughout Amis's mature work: see, for instance, *Einstein's Monsters*, *London Fields*, *Time's Arrow*, *Yellow Dog*.

[19] Martin Amis, 'Old Martin Amis Is in Your Face Again', interview (www.powells.com/authors/amis.html) (accessed 18 July 2008). All further references will be given in the text.

[20] Don DeLillo, *Mao II* (London: Jonathan Cape, 1992). In the words of de Lillo's protagonist, a reclusive novelist named Bill Gray, 'There's a curious knot that binds novelists and terrorists . . . Years ago I used to think it was possible for a novelist to alter the inner life of the culture. Now bomb-makers and gunmen have taken that territory. They make raids on human consciousness. What writers used to do before we were all incorporated . . . What terrorists gain, novelists lose', p. 41.

[21] Martin Amis, *Yellow Dog* (London: Vintage, 2003). All further references will be given in the text.

[22] Martin Amis, 'Posterity counts, Critics don't', interview, *Daily Telegraph*, 10 September, 2003. In Amis's words, 'I came back to *Yellow Dog* again after September 11 and I remember thinking . . . let's make this a comic novel, because, as well as rationality and morality, the whole notion of comedy had been put at risk. To me it felt like the end of the Age of Normalcy'.

[23] Jonathan Curiel, 'Martin Amis: Working with Words on all Fronts', *San Francisco Chronicle* 4 November 2001, p. 2.

[24] Gavin Keulks, 'W(h)ither Postmodernism? Late Amis', in *Martin Amis: Postmodernism and Beyond*, ed. by Gavin Keulks (London: Palgrave Macmillan, 2006), pp. 158–79. In Keulks's more generous view, *Yellow Dog*'s swerve into sanctimoniousness represents Amis's 'latest attempt to shock readers out of irony, detachment, and complacency', p. 176.

## CHAPTER THREE: PHILIP PULLMAN'S REPUBLIC OF HEAVEN

[1] Friedrich Nietzsche, *Twilight of the Idols and The Anti-Christ*, trans. by R. J. Hollingdale (London: Penguin, 1990), p. 33.

[2] Andrew Marr, 'Pullman does for atheism what C. S. Lewis did for God', *The Daily Telegraph*, 23 January 2002 (www.telegraph.co.uk/comment/3572210/Pullman-does-for-atheism-what-C-S-Lewis-did-for-God.html) (30 March 2009).

3 Philip Pullman, *The Amber Spyglass* (London: Scholastic, 2001), p. 464. All further references will be given in the text.

4 Philip Goodchild, *Capitalism and Religion: the Price of Piety* (London: Routledge, 2002), p. 17. All further references will be given in the text.

5 Peter Hitchens, 'This is the most dangerous author in Britain', *Mail on Sunday*, 27 January 2002. Also cited in Tony Watkins, *Dark Matter: A Thinking Fan's Guide to Philip Pullman* (Southampton: Damaris, 2004), p. 15.

6 Rowan Williams, 'A Near-Miraculous Triumph', *Guardian*, 10 March 2004 (www.guardian.co.uk/stage/2004/mar/10/theatre.religion (17 February 2009).

7 Books include those by Tony Watkins, cited above; Claire Squires, *Philip Pullman's His Dark Materials Trilogy: A Reader's Guide* (New York and London: Continuum, 2003); Nicholas Tucker, *Darkness Visible: Inside the World of Philip Pullman* (Cambridge: Wizard Books, 2003). All further references will be given in the text

8 Studies that focus specifically on the theological implications of the trilogy include Hugh Rayment-Pickard, *The Devil's Account: Philip Pullman and Christianity* (London: Darton, Longman and Todd, 2004); Donna Freitas and Jason King, *Killing the Impostor God: Philip Pullman's Spiritual Imagination in His Dark Materials* (San Francisco, CA: Jossey-Bass, 2007); Glenn Yeffeth ed. *Navigating the Golden Compass: Religion, Science and Daemonology in Philip Pullman's His Dark Materials* (Dallas, TX: Benbella Books, 2005). For more critical responses to the trilogy, see S. J. Masson, 'Philip Pullman's *His Dark Materials* Trilogy', *The Glass*, 15 (2003), 19–23, and Matthew Alderman, 'Whatever Happened to Susan Pevensie?', *First Things: the Journal of Religion, Culture and Public Life*, 17 February 2009. All further references will be given in the text.

9 'Every Indication of Inadvertent Solicitude' in *Richard Dawkins: How a Scientist Changed the Way We Think*, ed. by Alan Grafen and Mark Ridley (Oxford: Oxford University Press, 2006), pp. 270–6.

10 Alona Wartofsky, 'The Last Word', *Washington Post*, 19 February 2001. Quoted in Watkins, p. 15.

11 See Graham Holderness, '"The Undiscovered Country": Philip Pullman and the "Land of the Dead"', *Literature and Theology*, 21. 3 (2007), pp. 276–92. In this essay, Holderness evocatively describes Pullman as 'an anti-metaphysician who has, nonetheless, to adapt Nietzsche's phrase, lit his fire from the Christian flame' (p. 288). All further references will be given in the text.

12 On Pullman's antipathy for elements of the work of the famous literary scholar and Christian allegorist see, for example, his own article published in response to events celebrating the centenary of Lewis's birth, 'The Dark Side of Narnia', *Guardian*, 1 October 1998. See also Erica Wagner, 'Divinely Inspired: Philip Pullman', *The Times*, 18 October 2000 (www.ericawagner.co.uk/journalism.php?section=journalism2&id=14) (30 March 2009); John Ezard, 'Narnia books attacked as racist and sexist', *Guardian*, 2 June 2002 (www.guardian.co.uk/uk/2002/jun/03/gender.hayfestival2002) (30 March 2009).

[13] See, for example, Mikhail Bakhtin's highly influential study of the novel, *The Dialogic Imagination: Four Essays*, ed. by Michael Holquist, trans. by Caryl Emerson and Michael Holquist (Austin: University of Texas Press, 1981).

[14] John Milton, *Paradise Lost* (Oxford: Oxford University Press, 2005), Book I, l.1, p. 17. All further references will be given in the text.

[15] Michael Lieb, 'John Milton', in *The Blackwell Companion to the Bible in English Literature*, ed. by Rebecca Lemon, Emma Mason, Jonathan Roberts and Christopher Rowland (Oxford: Blackwell, 2009), pp. 269–85 (p. 282). All further references will be given in the text. See also Lieb's study, *Poetics of the Holy: A Reading of Paradise Lost* (Chapel Hill: University of North Carolina Press, 1981).

[16] See Watkins and Rayment-Pickard for detailed readings of the influence of Blake on Pullman.

[17] Introduction to *Paradise Lost*, p. 8. For a detailed exploration of the Romantic interpretation of Milton's poem, see Lucy Newlyn, *Paradise Lost and the Romantic Reader* (Oxford: Clarendon Press, 1993).

[18] Valentine Cunningham, 'Introduction: The Necessity of Heresy', in *Figures of Heresy: Radical Theology in English and American Writing*, ed. by Andrew Dix and Jonathan Taylor (Brighton: Sussex Academic Press, 2006), pp. 1–18.

[19] See, for example, G. R. Evans, *A Brief History of Heresy* (Oxford: Blackwell, 2003), p. 165.

[20] Peter Berger, *The Heretical Imperative: Contemporary Possibilities of Religious Affirmation* (London: Collins, 1980), pp. 28–31. Cited in Linda Woodhead and Paul Heelas, *Religion in Modern Times: An Interpretive Anthology* (Oxford: Blackwell, 2000), pp. 378–9.

[21] Callum G. Brown, *The Death of Christian Britain: Understanding Secularisation, 1800–2000* (London: Routledge, 2001), p. 193.

[22] C. S. Lewis, *A Preface to Paradise Lost* (London: Oxford University Press, 1971), p. 133. All further references will be given in the text.

[23] See also Lieb's views of Milton's Biblicism, *The Blackwell Companion to the Bible in English Literature*, p. 27.

[24] William Empson, *Milton's God* (London: Chatto and Windus, 1965), pp. 10–11. All further references will be given in the text.

[25] Bernard Schweizer also cites Empson's 'memorable words' of condemnation in his essay '"And he's A-Going to Destroy Him": Religious Subversion in Pullman's *His Dark Materials*', in *His Dark Materials Illuminated*, ed. by Millicent Lenz with Carole Scott (Detroit, MI: Wayne State University Press, 2005), pp. 160–73 (p. 168).

[26] Naomi Wood, 'Paradise Lost and Found: Obedience, Disobedience, and Storytelling in C. S. Lewis and Philip Pullman', *Children's Literature in Education*, 32. 4 (2001), pp. 237–59 (p. 248).

[27] Alan Jacobs, *Original Sin: A Cultural History* (London: SPCK, 2008), p. ix.

[28] Robert Butler, *Darkness Illuminated: Platform Discussions On 'His Dark Materials' at the National Theatre* (London: National Theatre/Oberon Books, 2004), p. 90. All further references will be given in the text.

[29] Philip Pullman, *Northern Lights* (London: Scholastic, 2001), p. 372. All further references will be given in the text.

[30] Naomi Wood, 'Dismembered Starlings and Neutered Minds', in *Navigating the Golden Compass: Religion, Science and Demonology in Philip Pullman's His Dark Materials*, ed. by Glenn Yeffeth (Dallas, TX: Benbella Books, 2005), pp. 15–23, p. 19. All further references will be given in the text.

[31] Philip Pullman, *The Subtle Knife* (London: Scholastic, 2001), p. 328. All further references will be given in the text.

[32] Friedrich, Nietzsche, *The Gay Science*, ed. by Walter Kauffman (New York: Vintage, 1974), §125, pp. 181–2.

[33] Terry Eagleton, *The Meaning of Life* (Oxford: Oxford University Press, 2007), p. 24. All further references will be given in the text.

[34] Nick Thorpe , 'Philip Pullman', *Times-Online*, 4 August 2002 (www.entertainment. timesonline.co.uk/tol/arts_and_entertainment/article1009649. ece?token=null&offset=12&page=2) (6 January 2008).

## CHAPTER FOUR: SALMAN RUSHDIE AND THE QUARREL OVER GOD

[1] Salman Rushdie, *The Enchantress of Florence*, p. 347. All further references will be given in the text.

[2] For a wide ranging discussion of the impact of the 'Rushdie Affair' see Kenan Malik, *From Fatwa to Jihad: The Rushdie Affair and Its Legacy* (London: Atlantic Books, 2009). See also Paul Weller, *A Mirror for Our Times: The Rushdie Affair and the Future of Multiculturalism* (London: Continuum, 2009).

[3] Graham Ward, *True Religion* (Oxford: Blackwell, 2003), p. 142. All further references will be in given in the text.

[4] The website of the Institute for Humanist Studies reported that following a ceremony at the Harvard Humanist Chaplaincy, honouring him for Outstanding Lifetime Achievement Award in Cultural Humanism, Rushdie claimed, in response to a question about the New Atheist movement that 'a little nuance wouldn't hurt' (25 April 2007) (http://humaniststudies.org/enews/?id=294&article=2) (accessed 10 May 2009).

[5] James Wood, 'An Exile's Sigh for Home' (Review of *The Ground Beneath Her Feet*), *Guardian*, 14 April 1999 (www.guardian.co.uk/GWeekly/Story/0,3939,308113,00.html) (14 April 2009). Wood suggests that Rushdie is 'the purest example' of the 'negative liberty' brought about by cultural, religious and national exile, the experience of being an *émigré*: 'literally homeless, he writes repeatedly about the actual and figurative centrifuges of modern life'.

[6] Ian Almond, *The New Orientalists: Postmodern Representations of Islam from Foucault to Baudrillard* (London: I. B. Tauris, 2007), p. 95. All further references will be given in the text. For an alternative reading of the spiritual themes of Rushdie's fiction, see Nicole M. Gyulay, '"Multiplicity Destroyed by Singularity": Salman Rushdie and Religious Hybridity', in *Spiritual Identities and the Post-Secular Imagination,* edited by Jo Carruthers and Andrew Tate (Oxford: Peter Lang, 2009).

[7] Salman Rushdie, *Imaginary Homelands: Essays and Criticism, 1981–1991*, p. 408. All further references will be given in the text.

[8] For a longer discussion of the science fiction and 'speculative fiction' experiments of *Grimus* and Rushdie's enthusiasm for the genre, see Andrew Teverson, *Salman Rushdie* (Manchester: Manchester University Press, 2007), pp. 111–35. All further references will be given in the text.

[9] Salman Rushdie, *The Ground beneath Her Feet* (London: Vintage, 2000), pp. 82–3. All further references will be given in the text.

[10] Michael Wood, 'The Orpheus of MTV' (*Review of The Ground Beneath Her Feet*), 18 April 1999 (www.nytimes.com/1999/04/18/books/the-orpheus-of-mtv.html) (14 April 2009).

[11] Salman Rushdie, *Shalimar the Clown* (London: Vintage, 2006), p. 6. All further references will be given in the text.

[12] Salman Rushdie, *Fury* (London: Vintage, 2002), pp. 47–8. All further references will be given in the text.

[13] The passage is quoted, for example, in John Updike's review of the novel, 'Paradises Lost', *The New Yorker*, 5 September 2005 (www.newyorker.com/archive /2005/09/05/050905crbo_books?printable=true); see also Johann Hari, 'Salman Rushdie: His Life, his Work and his religion', *Independent*, 13 October 2006 (www.independent.co.uk/news/people/profiles/salman-rushdie-his-life-his-work-and-his-religion-419902.html) (5 May 2009).

[14] Lee Siegel, 'Rushdie's Receding Talent' (Review of *Shalimar the Clown*), *The Nation*, 15 September 2005 (www.thenation.com/doc/20051003/siegel) (5 May 2009).

[15] Dominic Head, *The State of the Novel: Britain and Beyond* (Oxford: Blackwell, 2008), p. 95. Head also cites the quotation on the new global narrative from *Shalimar*, p. 37. All further references will be given in the text.

[16] Salman Rushdie, *Haroun and the Sea of Stories* (London: Penguin, 1991), p. 50. All further references will be given in the text.

[17] Salman Rushdie, 'In Defence of the Novel, Yet Again', in *Step across This Line: Collected Non-Fiction, 1992–2002* (London: Vintage, 2003), p. 58. All further references will be given in the text.

[18] Salman Rushdie, '"Imagine There's No Heaven": A Letter to the Six Billionth World Citizen' (originally published in 1997, updated and expanded for *The Portable Atheist: Essential Readings for the Non-Believer*, selected by Christopher Hitchens (London: Da Capo, 2007), pp. 380–3, p. 382. All further references will be given in the text.

## CONCLUSION: THE POST-ATHEIST NOVEL

[1] Friedrich Nietzsche, *The Genealogy of Morals*, Book 3, 24, trans. by Maudemarie Clark and Alan J. Swensen (Indianapolis, IN: Hackett, 1998), p. 110.

[2] Friedrich Nietzsche, *The Gay Science*, §125, p. 81. In this famous scene, Nietzsche writes: 'Have you not heard of that madman who lit a lantern in the bright morning hours, ran to the market place and cried

incessantly: "I seek God! I seek God!" – As many of those who did not believe in God were standing around just then, he provoked much laughter. Has he got lost? asked one. Did he lose his way like a child? asked another. Or is he hiding? Is he afraid of us? Has he gone on a voyage? emigrated? – Thus they yelled and laughed'.

3   For an account of 19th literary responses to the absence of God, see, for example, J. Hillis Miller, *The Disappearance of God: Five Nineteenth-Century Writers* (Cambridge: Belknap Press, 1975).

4   James Wood, *The Broken Estate: Essays in Literature and Belief* (London: Jonathan Cape, 1999), pp. xiv–xv. All further references will be given in the text.

5   James Wood, *The Book against God* (London: Vintage, 2004), p. 106.

6   John D. McClure, *Partial Faiths: Postsecular Fiction in the Age of Pynchon and Morrison* (Athens: University of Georgia Press, 2007), p. ix.

7   John Updike, *Seek My Face* (London: Penguin, 2002), p. 5.

8   Ian McEwan, 'Beyond the Bounds of Realism', *Guardian*, 31 January 2009, p. 2.

9   See Andrew Tate, *Contemporary Fiction and Christianity* (London: Continuum, 2008) for a larger survey of the reception of Christian theology in the contemporary Anglo-American novel.

# BIBLIOGRAPHY

## PRIMARY TEXTS

### Martin Amis

'Martin Amis: Working with Words on all Fronts', interview, *San Francisco Chronicle* 4 November 2001.

*The War Against Cliché: Essays and Reviews 1971–2000* (London: Jonathan Cape, 2001).

*Yellow Dog* (London: Vintage, 2003).

'Posterity Counts, Critics Don't', interview, *Daily Telegraph*, 10 September 2003.

'The Voice of Experience', interview, *The Times*, 9 September 2006.

'The Amis Papers', interview, *Observer*, 1 October 2006.

'30 Things I've Learned about Terror', interview, *Independent*, 8 October 2006.

'Martin Amis: You Ask the Questions', interview, *Independent*, 15 January 2007.

Martin Amis, 'Old Martin Amis Is in Your Face Again', interview (www.powells.com/authors/amis.html) (18 July 2008).

'The Two Faces of Amis', interview, *Independent*, 29 January 2008.

*The Second Plane: September 11: 2001–2007* (London: Jonathan Cape, 2008).

### Ian McEwan

*The Child in Time* (London: Vintage, 1987).

*Black Dogs* (London: Vintage, 1992).

*Enduring Love* (London: Vintage, 1997).

'Move Over, Darwin', *Guardian*, 20 September 1998.

'Only Love then Oblivion: Love Was All They Had to Set against Their Murderers', *Guardian*, 15 September 2001 (www.guardian.co.uk/world/2001/sep/15/september11.politicsphilosophyandsociety2).

*Atonement* (London: Vintage, 2002).

*Saturday* (London: Vintage, 2005).

'A Parallel Tradition', *Guardian*, 1 April 2006.

'Ian McEwan: I Hang on to Hope in a Tide of Fear', interview, *Independent*, 7 April 2007.

'End of the World Blues', in *The Portable Atheist: Essential Readings for the Non-Believer*, ed. by Christopher Hitchens (London: Da Capo Press, 2007), pp. 351–65.

*On Chesil Beach* (London: Jonathan Cape, 2007).

'The TNR Q & A: Ian McEwan on Bellow, the Internet, Atheism, and Why His Books Are Still Scary', interview, *New Republic*, 11 January 2008.

Interview, Random House Readers' Group Reading Guides (www.random-house.co.uk/readersgroup/readingguide.htm?command=Search&db=/catalog/main.txt&eqisbndata=0099429799#interview) (1 May 2008).

'McEwan et L'Islamismo: "Lo disprezzo"', *Corriere della Sera*, 21 June 2008.

'Beyond the Bounds of Realism', *Guardian*, 31 January 2009, p. 2.

## Philip Pullman

'The Dark Side of Narnia', *Guardian*, 1 October 1998.

*The Amber Spyglass* (London: Scholastic, 2001).

*Northern Lights* (London: Scholastic, 2001).

*The Subtle Knife* (London: Scholastic, 2001).

'Every Indication of Inadvertent Solicitude', in *Richard Dawkins: How a Scientist Changed the Way We Think*, ed. by Alan Grafen and Mark Ridley (Oxford: Oxford University Press, 2006), pp. 270–6.

## Salman Rushdie

*Haroun and the Sea of Stories* (London: Penguin, 1991).

*Imaginary Homelands: Essays and Criticism, 1981–1991* (London: Granta, 1991).

*The Ground beneath Her Feet* (London: Vintage, 2000).

*Fury* (London: Vintage, 2002).

'In Defence of the Novel, Yet Again', in *Step across This Line: Collected Non-Fiction, 1992–2002* (London: Vintage, 2003).

*Shalimar the Clown* (London: Vintage, 2006).

'"Imagine There's No Heaven": A Letter to the Six Billionth World Citizen' (originally published in 1997, updated and expanded for *The Portable Atheist: Essential Readings for the Non-Believer*, ed. by Christopher Hitchens (London: Da Capo, 2007), pp. 380–3.

*The Enchantress of Florence* (London: Jonathan Cape, 2008).

## SECONDARY TEXTS

Alderman, Matthew, 'Whatever Happened to Susan Pevensie?', *First Things: The Journal of Religion, Culture and Public Life*, 17 February 2009 (www.firstthings.com/onthesquare/2009/02/whatever-happened-to-susan-pev) (9 April 2009).

## BIBLIOGRAPHY

Almond, Ian, *The New Orientalists: Postmodern Representations of Islam from Foucault to Baudrillard* (London: I. B. Tauris, 2007).

Bakhtin, Mikhail, *The Dialogic Imagination: Four Essays*, ed. by Michael Holquist and trans. by Caryl Emerson and Michael Holquist (Austin: University of Texas Press, 1981).

Baudrillard, Jean, *The Spirit of Terrorism and Requiem for the Twin Towers*, trans. by Chris Turner (London: Verso, 2002).

Beattie, Tina, *The New Atheists: The Twilight of Reason and the War on Religion* (London: Darton, Longman & Todd, 2007).

Berger, Peter, *The Heretical Imperative: Contemporary Possibilities of Religious Affirmation* (London: Collins, 1980).

Bhabha, Homi K., 'Terror and After . . . ', *Parallax* 1 (2002): pp. 3–4.

Bradley, Arthur, 'The New Atheist Novel: Literature, Religion and Terror in Amis and McEwan', in *The Yearbook of English Studies 2009*, special issue on Literature and Religion, ed. by Andrew Tate (New York: MHRA, 2009).

Brown, Callum G., *The Death of Christian Britain: Understanding Secularisation, 1800–2000* (London: Routledge, 2001).

Butler, Robert, *Darkness Illuminated: Platform Discussions on 'His Dark Materials' at the National Theatre* (London: National Theatre/Oberon Books, 2004).

Clark, Roger and Gordon, Andy, *Ian McEwan's 'Enduring Love'* (London: Continuum, 2003).

Cornwell, John, *Darwin's Angel: A Seraphic Response to* The God Delusion (London: Profile, 2007).

Cunningham, Valentine, 'Introduction: The Necessity of Heresy', in *Figures of Heresy: Radical Theology in English and American Writing*, ed. by Andrew Dix and Jonathan Taylor (Brighton: Sussex Academic Press, 2006), pp. 1–18.

Dalrymple, Theodore, 'What the New Atheists Don't See', *City Journal*, Autumn 2007 (www.city-journal.org/html/17_4_oh_to_be.html) (5 January 2009).

Darwin, Charles, *The Origin of Species* (New York: Gramercy Books, 1979 [1859]), p. 459.

Dawkins, Richard, *The Selfish Gene* (Oxford: Oxford University Press, 1989 [1976]).

–, *Unweaving the Rainbow: Science, Delusion and the Appetite for Wonder* (London: Allen Lane/The Penguin Press, 1998).

–, *The God Delusion* (London: Transworld, 2nd edition 2006).

DeLillo, Don, *Mao II* (London: Jonathan Cape, 1992).

Dennett, Daniel C., *Breaking the Spell: Religion as a Natural Phenomenon* (London: Allen Lane, 2006).

Derrida, Jacques and Borradori, Giovanna, 'Autoimmunity: Real and Symbolic Suicides', in *Philosophy in a Time of Terror: Dialogues with Jacques Derrida and Jurgen Habermas*, ed. by Giovanna Borradori (Chicago: University of Chicago Press, 2003), pp. 85–136.

Dershowitz, Alan, *The Case for Israel* (Hoboken, NJ: John Wiley, 2003).

Eagleton, Terry, 'Lunging, Flailing, Mispunching' (Review of *The God Delusion*), *London Review of Books*, 19 October 2006.

–, *The Meaning of Life* (Oxford: Oxford University Press, 2007).

–, *Reason, Faith and God: Reflections on the God Debate* (New Haven, CT: Yale University Press, 2009).

Empson, William, *Milton's God* (London: Chatto and Windus, 1965).

Evans, G. R., *A Brief History of Heresy* (Oxford: Blackwell, 2003).

Ezard, John, 'Narnia Books Attacked as Racist and Sexist', *Guardian*, 2 June 2002 (www.guardian.co.uk/uk/2002/jun/03/gender.hayfestival2002) (30 March 2009).

Fischer, Tibor, 'A Tour of Stalin's Labour Camps' (Review of *House of Meetings*), *Daily Telegraph*, 11 October 2006.

Freitas, Donna and King, Jason, *Killing the Impostor God: Philip Pullman's Spiritual Imagination in His Dark Materials* (San Francisco, CA: Jossey-Bass, 2007).

Frow, John, 'The Uses of Terror and the Limits of Cultural Studies', *Symploke* 11, 1–2 (2003), pp. 69–76.

Goodchild, Philip, *Capitalism and Religion: the Price of Piety* (London: Routledge, 2002).

Gray, John, *Black Mass: Apocalyptic Religion and the Death of Utopia* (London: Allen Lane, 2007).

Grayling, A. C., *Against All Gods: Six Polemics on Religion and an Essay on Kindness* (London: Oberon, 2007).

Gyulay, Nicole M., '" Multiplicity Destroyed by Singularity": Salman Rushdie and Religious Hybridity', in *Spiritual Identities: Literature and the Post-Secular Imagination* (Oxford: Peter Lang, 2009).

Hari, Johann, 'Salman Rushdie: His Life, His Work and His religion', *Independent*, 13 October 2006 (www.independent.co.uk/news/people/profiles/salman-rushdie-his-life-his-work-and-his-religion-419902.html) (5 May 2009).

Harpham, Geoffrey Galt, 'Symbolic Terror', *Critical Inquiry* 28 (Winter 2002), pp. 573–9.

Harris, Sam, *The End of Faith: Religion, Terror and the Future of Reason* (New York: W. W. Norton, 2004).

–, *Letter to a Christian Nation: A Challenge to the Faith of America* (London: Bantam, 2007).

Hayes, M. Hunter, 'A Reluctant Leavisite: Martin Amis's "Higher Journalism"', in *Martin Amis: Postmodernism and Beyond*, ed. by Gavin Keulks (Basingstoke: Palgrave Macmillan, 2006), pp. 197–210.

Hayles, N. Katherine, *How We Became Posthuman: Virtual Bodies in Cybernetics, Literature and Informatics* (Chicago: University of Chicago Press, 1999).

Head, Dominic, *Ian McEwan*, Contemporary British Novelists (Manchester: Manchester University Press, 2007).

–, *The State of the Novel: Britain and Beyond* (Oxford: Blackwell, 2008).

Hitchens, Christopher, 'On the Frontiers of Apocalypse', in *Love, Poverty and War: Journeys and Essays* (London: Atlantic, 2005).

–, *God is Not Great: The Case against Religion* (London: Atlantic Books, 2007).

–, ed. *The Portable Atheist: Essential Readings for the Non-Believer* (London: Da Capo Press, 2007).

Hitchens, Peter, 'This is the Most Dangerous Author in Britain', *Mail on Sunday*, 27 January 2002.

Holderness, Graham, '"The Undiscovered Country": Philip Pullman and the "Land of the Dead"', *Literature and Theology*, 21. 3 (2007), pp. 276–92.

Houen, Alex, *Terrorism and Modern Literature: From Joseph Conrad to Ciaran Carson* (Oxford: Oxford University Press, 2002).

Huntington, Samuel P., *The Clash of Civilisations and the Remaking of World Order* (New York: Simon & Schuster, 1988).

Jacobs, Alan, *Original Sin: A Cultural History* (London: SPCK, 2008).

–, 'Amis Amiss', *First Things: The Journal of Religion, Culture and Public Life* (June/July, 2008) (www.firstthings.com/article.php3?id_article=6236) (31 January 2009).

Kant, Immanuel, 'An Answer to the Question: What is Enlightenment?', in *Kant's Political Writings*, trans. by H. B. Nisbet, ed. by Hans Reiss (Cambridge: Cambridge University Press, 1970), pp. 54–60.

Keulks, Gavin, 'W(h)ither Postmodernism? Late Amis', in *Martin Amis: Postmodernism and Beyond*, ed. by Gavin Keulks (London: Palgrave Macmillan, 2006), pp. 158–79.

Lentricchia, Frank and McAuliffe, Jody, *Crimes of Art + Terror* (Chicago and London: University of Chicago Press, 2003).

Lewis, C. S., *A Preface to* Paradise Lost (London: Oxford University Press, 1971).

Lieb, Michael, *Poetics of the Holy: A Reading of Paradise Lost* (Chapel Hill: University of North Carolina Press, 1981).

–, 'John Milton', in *The Blackwell Companion to the Bible in English Literature*, ed. by Rebecca Lemon, Emma Mason, Jonathan Roberts and Christopher Rowland (Oxford: Blackwell, 2009), pp. 269–85.

Lukács, Georg, *Theory of the Novel: A Historico-Philosophical Essay in the Forms of Great Epic Literature*, trans. by A. Bostock (Cambridge, MA: MIT, 1971).

Malik, Kenan, *From Fatwa to Jihad: The Rushdie Affair and Its Legacy* (London: Atlantic Books, 2009).

Marr, Andrew, 'Pullman Does for Atheism What C. S. Lewis Did for God', *Daily Telegraph*, 23 January 2002 (www.telegraph.co.uk/comment/3572210/Pullman-does-for-atheism-what-C-S-Lewis-did-for-God.html) (30 March 2009).

Masson, S. J., 'Philip Pullman's *His Dark Materials* Trilogy', *The Glass* 15 (2003), 19–23.

Matar, Nabil, ed. *In the Lands of the Christians: Arabic Travel Writing in the Seventeenth Century* (London: Routledge, 2003).

McClure, John D., *Partial Faiths: Postsecular Fiction in the Age of Pynchon and Morrison* (Athens: University of Georgia Press, 2007).

McGrath, Alastair and Collicutt McGrath, Joanna, *The Dawkins Delusion? Atheist Fundamentalism and the Denial of the Divine* (London: SPCK, 2007).

Midgely, Mary, *Evolution as a Religion: Strange Hopes and Stranger Fears* (London and New York: Routledge, 2002).

Miller, J. Hillis, *The Disappearance of God: Five Nineteenth-Century Writers* (Cambridge: Belknap Press, 1975).

Milton, John, *Paradise Lost* (Oxford: Oxford University Press, 2005).

Newlyn, Lucy, *Paradise Lost and the Romantic Reader* (Oxford: Clarendon Press, 1993).

Nietzsche, Friedrich, *The Gay Science*, ed. by Walter Kauffman (New York: Vintage, 1974).

–, *Twilight of the Idols and the Anti-Christ*, trans. by R. J. Hollingdale (London: Penguin, 1990).

–, *The Genealogy of Morals*, trans. by Maudemarie Clark and Alan J. Swensen (Indianapolis, IN: Hackett, 1998).

Onfray, Michel, *Traité d'athéologie: Physique de la métaphysique*, Paris, Grasset, (2005), trans. by Jeremy Leggatt as *Atheist Manifesto: The Case against Christianity, Judaism, and Islam* (New York: Arcade, 2007).

Pape, Robert, *Dying to Win: The Strategic Logic of Suicide Terrorism* (New York: Random House, 2005).

Paulhan, Jean, *The Flowers of Tarbes, or Terror in Literature*, trans. by Michael Syrotinski (Chicago: Illinois University Press, 2006 [1936]).

Perloff, Marjorie, 'Martin Amis and the Boredom of Terror' (Review of *The Second Plane*), *Times Literary Supplement*, 13 February 2008.

Rayment-Pickard, Hugh, *The Devil's Account: Philip Pullman and Christianity* (London: Darton, Longman and Todd, 2004).

Ricoeur, Paul, *Memory, History, Forgetting*, trans. by Kathleen Blamey & David Pellauer (Chicago: University of Chicago Press, 2006).

Ridley, Matt, 'Richard Dawkins and the Golden Pen', in *Richard Dawkins: How a Scientist Changed the Way We Think*, ed. by Alan Grafen and Mark Ridley (Oxford: Oxford University Press, 2007), pp. 265–9.

Ross, Andrew, *The Chicago Gangster Theory of Life* (London: Verso, 1994).

Roy, Olivier, *Globalised Islam: The Search for a New Umma* (London: Hurst, 2004).

Sardar, Ziauddin, 'Welcome to Planet Blitcon', *New Statesman*, 11 December 2006.

Scanlan, Margaret, *Plotting Terror: Novelists and Terrorists in Contemporary Fiction* (Charlottesville: University of Virginia Press, 2001).

Schweizer, Bernard, '"And he's A-Going to Destroy Him": Religious Subversion in Pullman's *His Dark Materials*', in *His Dark Materials Illuminated*, ed. by Millicent Lenz with Carole Scott (Detroit, MI: Wayne State University Press, 2005), pp. 160–73.

Siegel, Lee, 'Rushdie's Receding Talent' (Review of *Shalimar the Clown*), *Nation*, 15 September 2005 (www.thenation.com /doc/20051003/siegel) (5 May 2009).

Southern, R. W., *Western Views of Islam in the Middle Ages* (Cambridge, MA: Harvard University Press, 1965).

Squires, Claire, *Philip Pullman's His Dark Materials Trilogy: A Reader's Guide* (New York and London: Continuum, 2003).

Stockhausen, Karlheinz, 'Huuuh! Das Pressegespräch am 16. September 2001 im Senatszimmer des Hotel Atlantic in Hamburg', *MusikTexte* 91 (2002), pp. 69–77.

Tait, Theo, 'A Rational Diagnosis' (Review of *Saturday*), *Times Literary Supplement*, 11 February 2005, pp. 21–2.

Tate, Andrew, *Contemporary Fiction and Christianity* (London: Continuum, 2008).

Terranova, Tiziana, *Network Culture: Politics for the Information Age* (London: Pluto, 2004).

Teverson, Andrew, *Salman Rushdie* (Manchester: Manchester University Press, 2007).

Thorpe, Nick, 'Philip Pullman', *Times-Online*, 4 August 2002 (www. entertainment.timesonline.co.uk/tol/arts_and_entertainment/article1009649.ece?token=null&offset=12&page=2) (6 January 2008).

Tucker, Nicholas, *Darkness Visible: Inside the World of Philip Pullman* (Cambridge: Wizard Books, 2003).

Unger, Craig, *The Fall of the House of Bush: The Delusions of the Neo-Conservatives and American Armageddon* (London: Pocket, 2008).

Updike, John, *Seek My Face* (London: Penguin, 2002).

–, 'Paradises Lost' (Review of *Shalimar the Clown*), *New Yorker*, 5 September 2005. (www.newyorker.com/archive/2005/09/05/050905crbo_books?printable=true) (5 May 2009).

Virilio, Paul, *Ground Zero*, trans. by Chris Turner (London: Verso, 2002).

Wagner, Erica, 'Divinely Inspired: Philip Pullman', *The Times*, 18 October 2000 (www.ericawagner.co.uk/journalism.php?section=journalism2&id=14) (30 March 2009).

Ward, Graham, *True Religion* (Oxford: Blackwell, 2003).

Wartofsky, Alona, 'The Last Word', *Washington Post*, 19 February 2001.

Watkins, Tony, *Dark Matter: A Thinking Fan's Guide to Philip Pullman* (Southampton: Damaris, 2004).

Weller, Paul, *A Mirror for Our Times: The Rushdie Affair and the Future of Multiculturalism* (London: Continuum, 2009).

Williams, Rowan, 'A Near-Miraculous Triumph', *Guardian*, 10 March 2004 (www.guardian.co.uk/stage/2004/mar/10/theatre.religion) (17 February 2009).

Wood, James, 'Why It All Adds Up' (Review of *Enduring Love*), *Guardian*, 4 December 1997, pp. 9–10

–, *The Broken Estate: Essays in Literature and Belief* (London: Jonathan Cape, 1999).

–, *The Book against God* (London: Vintage, 2004).

–, 'On a Darkling Plain: Ian McEwan's *Saturday*', *New Republic*, 14 April 2005.

–, 'An Exile's Sigh for Home' (Review of *The Ground beneath Her Feet*), *Guardian*, 14 April 1999 (www.guardian.co.uk/GWeekly/Story/0,3939,308113,00.Html) (14 April 2009).

Wood, Michael, 'The Orpheus of MTV' (Review of *The Ground beneath Her Feet*), 18 April 1999 (www.nytimes.com/1999/04/18/books/the-orpheus-of-mtv.html) (14 April 2009).

Wood, Naomi, 'Paradise Lost and Found: Obedience, Disobedience, and Storytelling in C. S. Lewis and Philip Pullman', *Children's Literature in Education* 32. 4 (2001), pp. 237–59.

–, 'Dismembered Starlings and Neutered Minds', in *Navigating the Golden Compass: Religion, Science and Demonology in Philip Pullman's His Dark Materials*, ed. by Glenn Yeffeth (Dallas, TX: Benbella Books, 2005), pp. 15–23.

Woodhead, Linda and Heelas, Paul, *Religion in Modern Times: An Interpretive Anthology* (Oxford: Blackwell, 2000).

Žižek, Slavoj, *Welcome to the Desert of the Real* (London: Verso, 2003).

# INDEX

Almond, Ian 84
Amis, Martin
  account of the Muslim
    religion 42
  champion of secular
    enlightenment 36
  definition of 'literature' 44
  essay on Saul Bellow 38
  'The Last Days of Mohammed
    Atta' (2006) 49
  literature against religion 39
  literature as the object for secular
    devotion 37
  *Money* (1984) 50
  'In the Palace of the End'
    (2004) 49
  post-9/11 fiction/literature 50, 53
  *The Second Plane* (2008) 12, 13,
    37, 40–3, 49, 50
  'Terror and Boredom' (2002) 30
  *Time's Arrow* 45
  views on literature 37
  views on September 11 41, 46,
    47
  'The Voice of the Lonely Crowd'
    (2002) 36, 40
  and the war for cliché 36–55
  *Yellow Dog* 49, 52
Amis/Eagleton spat 53
Arnold, Mathew 37
  'Dover Beach' 32
atheist tyrannies of the twentieth
  century 3

Auster, Paul 96
Ayatollah Khomeini 45

Berman, Paul 30, 42
Brontë, Charlotte 71
Bush, George W. 4

Dawkins, Richard 1–10, 13, 14, 17,
    37, 56, 58, 111
  *The God Delusion* (2006) 1, 2, 4,
    5, 9
  and his fellow atheists 7
  human beings as nothing but
    gene machines 8
  as a Pentecostalist evangelist 5
DeLillo, Don 50
Dennett, Daniel 1–3, 8, 9, 10, 14
  *Breaking the Spell* (2006) 1
Dickens, Charles 71

Eagleton, Terry 76, 106
Enlightenment tradition 2

Freitas, Donna 58
Freud, Sigmund 74
Fuentes, Carlos 95

Gray, John 2, 8

Harris, Sam 2, 3, 5, 6, 8, 14, 30, 42
  diatribe 4
  *The End of Faith* 1, 5, 7
Head, Dominic 92, 94

Hitchens, Christopher 1–3, 5, 6, 9, 10, 14, 18, 30, 37, 42
  *God Is Not Great* (2007) 1, 6, 10
Hitchens, Peter 71

Joyce, James' *Ulysses* 39

Kant, Immanuel 2
King, Jason 58
Koresh, David 17
Kundera, Milan 96

Larkin, Philip 18, 38
  'Aubade' 18
Leavis, F. R. 37, 42
Lewis, Bernard 3, 30, 42
Lewis, C. S. 13
  *The Chronicles of Narnia* (1950–6) 59
  *The Last Battle* (1956) 79
  Narnia series 13
Lindh, John Walker 49
London suicide bombings of July 2005 5
Lovelock, James 37
Lucas, George
  *Star Wars* (1977–83) 59
Lukács, Georg 10, 72
  *Theory of the Novel* 72
Luther, Martin 49

Malone, Mary 72
Marx, Karl 74
McClure, John D. 109
McEwan, Ian 10, 14, 16–35, 42, 58, 107, 111
  2002 interview about his novel *Atonement* 23
  *Atonement* (2002) 12, 21, 23, 24, 25, 26, 27
  belief in the redemptive powers of the literary 22
  *Black Dogs* (1992) 18, 19, 20, 21

*On Chesil Beach* (2007) 10, 12, 34, 35
  critic of the supposed fripperies of postmodern relativism 21
  'End of the World Blues' (2007) 17, 18, 29, 34, 35, 37, 42
  *Enduring Love* (1997) 19, 20, 21, 31
  famous coda to McEwan's novel 26, 27
  fiction 12
  the idea of the moral imagination 25
  'Islamism' 22
  a New Atheist novelist 16, 17
  novelist-as-narcissist 26
  novelist's moral imagination 27
  'Only Love Then Oblivion' 22, 24, 25
  post-9/11 fiction 21, 23
  profession of faith in McEwan's fiction 16
  *Saturday* (2005) 10, 12, 21, 23, 28, 29, 30, 33
  *The Trials of Arabella* 25
Midgely, Mary 7
Milton, John 13
  *Paradise Lost* (1667) 13, 62, 81
*mythopoeia*
  of New Atheism 7, 9

'New Atheism' 1, 7
  aesthetics 9
  and Christian fundamentlism 3–4
  distinction from earlier varieties of non-belief 2
  literary reception 2
  'meme' 3
  as a response to a very specific cultural and political climate 3
New Atheist novel 11, 12, 14, 15, 103, 105

belief system 97
future 111
Islamism 42
New Atheist novelists 61, 107
'Atheist Delusion' 106
representation of 'Islam' 30
New Atheists 2, 8
creation myth 7
first polemics 3
and Islam 5
and *literature* 10
popularity of their work 2
process of self-replication 3
Nietzsche, Friedrich 56, 74, 106
*The Gay Science* 74, 106
'metaphysical faith' 106

Osama Bin Laden 40, 41, 46, 47

Perloff, Marjorie 41
Pinter, Harold 94
post-atheist fiction 109
Pullman, Philip 11, 111
*The Amber Spyglass* (2000) 57,
61, 70, 72, 77
an anti-Christian
propagandist 58
argument against transcendent
religion 57
controversial trilogy 13
*His Dark Materials* (1995–2000)
13, 56, 61, 71, 76, 94, 107
killing off God 75
and Milton's *Paradise Lost*
(1667) 62
New Atheist novel 80
*Northern Lights* (1995) 57, 62, 71
Republic of Heaven 56–81
*The Subtle Knife* (1997) 57, 60,
70, 71

Rayment-Pickard, Hugh 59, 80
The Devil's Account 80

Ricoeur, Paul 40
Rilke's *Sonnets to Orpheus* 87
Rumsfeld, Donald 54
Rushdie, Salman *see* Salman
Rushdie
'Rushdie affair' 83, 94
Russell, Bertrand 3

Salman Rushdie 107, 111
The *Enchantress of Florence*
(2008) 14, 81, 86, 94
epigram from *Romeo and
Juliet* 90
*fatwa* 13, 83, 87, 94
fiction of faith 85
fiction of the early twenty first
century 88
*Fury* (2001) 88, 89, 90, 92, 93,
102
'In God We Trust' 98
'In Good Faith' (1990) 85
*Grimus* (1975) 86, 98
*The Ground beneath Her Feet*
(1999) 82, 86, 87, 88, 92,
99, 100
*Haroun and the Sea of Stories*
(1990) 94, 95
*Imaginary Homelands* (1992) 85,
95, 98, 99, 100
'Is Nothing Sacred?' 94
letter addressed to 'the Six
Billionth World Citizen' 98
'malevolent Divine' 101
*Midnight's Children* (1981) 92
motif of unexpected epiphany
87
*post-Satanic Verses* fiction 84
and the quarrel over God
82–104
religious scepticism in
contemporary anglophone
fiction 84
*The Satanic Verses* (1988) 13, 83

Salman Rushdie (*Cont'd*)
  *Shalimar the Clown* (2005)  88, 90,
    93, 94, 96, 97, 98, 99
  *Step Across This Line* (2002)  96
  treatment of *homo fabulans*  92
*The Satanic Verses* (1988)  13,
    see *also* New Atheist novel
Sayyid Qutb's *Milestones*  41
Shklovsky, Viktor  47
Siegel, Lee  92, 93
Steiner, George  96
Steyn, Mark  42, 49
'strong man' theory of
    nation-building  6
suicide bomber  5
  as the logical conclusion of the
    Muslim creed  5
  Palestinian  5

Tait, Theo  21
Thorpe, Nick  80
Tolkein, J. R. R.  59

Updike, John  110
  *In the Beauty of the Lilies*
    (1997)  110
  *Seek My Face* (2002)  110

Ward, Graham  83
War on Terror  6
Williams, Rowan Dr  57
Winthrop, John  93
*The Wizard of Oz*  59
Wood, James  22, 33, 84, 108
  *The Book against God* (2003)
    108
  *The Broken Estate*  108
  deracination as a vital element
    of Rushdie's creative
    focus  84
  'On a Darkling Plain'  33
Wood, Michael  86
Wood, Naomi  79

Ziauddin Sardar  40